Indian Sweet Cookery

By the same author:

Indian Vegetarian Cookery
Traditional Indian Cookery

OM. To the Mother of all cooks

Sometimes She is known as Madhumati—Honey
(Lalitāsahasranāman)

Indian Sweet Cookery

Jack Santa Maria

Illustrated by Carmen Miranda

Shambhala Boulder 1980

Shambhala Publications, Inc.
1123 Spruce Street
Boulder, Colorado 80302

Distributed in the United States of America by Random House

Printed in the United States of America

LIBRARY OF CONGRESS CATALOGING IN PUBLICATION DATA

Santa Maria, Jack.
Indian sweet cookery.

1. Desserts. 2. Cookery, India. I. Title.
TX773.S315 641.8′6 79-67689
ISBN 0-87773-176-4 pbk.
ISBN 0-394-73880-2 (Random House)

Contents

Acknowledgements

The author wishes to thank Ann and Bury Peerless
for permission to reproduce the cover illustration.

Special thanks are also due to the following:
My numerous teachers.
Mrs Eunice Santa Maria, for her recipes and help during many stages of the preparation.
The late Mrs Biriani, with fond memories.
Mrs Esther Ezekiel, for her recipe and expert demonstration.
Mrs T. M. B. Nedungadi, for her South Indian recipes and helpful information on temple offerings.
Kevin McDermott, my editor, for his continuous support and help.
Bhagavan Soaham, for his loving guidance.
The Royal Asiatic Society.

Food for the Gods

'Jaggery, payasam, ghee, appam, modakam, curds, dal, all these are to be offered as Food for the Gods (*naivadiyam*).'
(Lord Krishna in Skanda XI, *Bhagavata Purāna*)

If we want to please a child we offer sweets. Often a friendship may begin this way. The giving of the sweet is an act of friendship, affection or love. In the words of love, images of sweetness are used to describe the loved one so that sweets may so easily symbolize this bond.

For thousands of years, the Hindus have sought to please the gods and goddesses by showing their devotion through the offering of sweet things to eat and drink, see, smell and touch. In the sacred scriptures it is said that the gods and goddesses are like children because they take delight in simple offerings, especially sweet ones. The *Devi Bhagavata Purāna* describes Brahman in the form of Devi, the Goddess. When she is discerned in the Manipura Lotus, or the navel centre of the body, it says that she takes the form of *Lākini* who is fond of sweetmeats and does good to all (IV). Hence the scriptures assure the devotee that sweet food is a welcome offering at all times. Puja, the private daily act of worship, is central to Hindu life. Among such things as incense, flowers and fruit, sweets are an important part of the offerings made to the god, goddess or Chosen Ideal of the worshipper. Indeed, the worshipper's idea of the sacred is said to reside in the centre of a sea of nectar, the thousand-petalled lotus where the individual self (*ātman*) and the cosmic self (Brahman) are seen as one. This union is frequently compared to the taste of honey or some divine nectar. Sometimes the same image is described as a beautiful city to be found on a jewelled island which is itself set in an ocean of sweet milk.

This nectar gives its name to the special offering and libation made by the priests. It is used to bathe an image or object during the puja.

Such a nectar (*amrita*) is usually made from five ingredients such as honey, milk, ghee, sugar and water and is known as *pānchamrita*. Sometimes the feet of holy men and women are washed in the panchamrita as a form of worship. In this special offering are found the basic ingredients of all Indian sweets and the essential reason for using them. Blended with these ingredients are fruits and vegetables, spices and aromatics, nuts and beautiful garnishes, according to traditional and local ways. Thus in different parts of the country, the same basic dish may be found with almost similar ingredients but bearing a different local name and usually having its own distinct qualities. No wonder that an amazing variety of sweets is found today in India.

But they were never created to satisfy taste alone. They are primarily intended as a source of food so that they are good enough for the highest ideal of the sacred. Sugar, honey, milk, nuts, spices and perfumes are used as a seduction or encouragement to take wholesome nourishment. Being food for the gods, they are indeed foods for promoting health and well-being, and the cook must ensure that only the best ingredients are used whenever possible. According to the Yogis of ancient times, food, like other matter, may be classified according to the three qualities it possesses. They advise us to avoid or cut down the consumption of too much food which contains the qualities of *tamas*, inertia, or *rajas*, activity. Rather, they suggest, food which contains the quality of *sattva*, harmony, should be taken. Sattvic food helps those pursuing a life of Yoga or meditation, or anyone who is trying to bring more harmony into the life-style. It will be found that the sweets in this book, if carefully prepared, have this essential sattvic quality described in the *Bhagavad Gītā* (see Discourse XVII).*

Hardly a day goes by in India which is not special because of its association with a god or goddess or some aspect of Hindu religion. Hindus celebrate hundreds of sacred occasions with festive observances. Many are seasonal, celebrating harvest or fertility. Heavenly bodies such as the moon and stars, eclipses, solstices, equinoxes, all figure in the round of celebrations. Some honour the gods and goddesses or commemorate their birth or the victory of some heroic character. Such days are often named after the personality concerned. Shivaratra, for example, the Night of Shiva, is observed by devotees of Shiva throughout the country. Festivals generally last about a week though they may go on for two weeks to a month. But a long festival is expen-

*Further discussion about food and the three qualities (*gūnas*) of matter in Hindu philosophy will be found in *Indian Vegeṭarian Cookery* (Rider, 1973), p. 19.

sive and only the people of a large town or prosperous village are able to afford it. Hindus use the Moon calendar. Months are calculated according to the phases of the Moon and are therefore moveable. Apart from the regular festivals which are celebrated according to the Moon calendar, there is no calendar regulating the festivals or forms of worship for the village deities. In some villages where there is a permanent shrine, offerings of rice, fruit, sweets and flowers, with incense and camphor, are made every day by the villagers.

Although most sweets are made all the year round, some holidays require that a special dish shall be made for that day and some have become in the course of time associated with certain gods or goddesses. They like these particular dishes served on their special days. For example, *Agrayanam* or *Navānnapornima* is the full-moon day on which the new harvest food has to be tasted. On this day the family deities are offered special worship at which the goddess Lakshmi always presides. Rice is boiled with milk and sugar to make *kshīr* or *khīr* which is then offered to Lakshmi and the family deities. Then it will be eaten as the special dainty of the day. (Some recipes for khir and other dishes like it will be found in the section entitled *Puddings*.) Perhaps in a country which is the third largest producer of sugar in the world, it is not surprising to find so many traditions associated with it. Since ancient times it has been considered auspicious to feed other beings with sweet things. Sugar is still scattered on ant-hills and this act is said to bring great merit. Indeed, in parts of Western India both honey and sweetmeats are considered capable of absorbing evil thoughts and vibrations and to nullify them thereby. Who knows what giving a few sugar lumps to your favourite horse may bring!

So, as well as love and devotion, sweets certainly mean fun and festivity. Can there be a family which does not have some aunty, old granny or interesting relation who serves as the repository of a secret sweet recipe? These special people, the friends of all children, have preserved and treasured some delicacy like gold, carefully coffered in the vaults of memory. Festival time comes round and suddenly ordinary people take on the air of magicians. Their true role in life is revealed. The whole family and perhaps the neighbours too, eagerly await the arrival of the sweets. Of course, part of the fun in waiting is the certain knowledge that so and so always makes it perfectly – like no one else can! So high is the art of cooking esteemed that in some parts of the country children are named after many of the vital ingredients in sweet-making. In Gujerat, for example, among common children's names are Gulab, from *gulab*, a rose; Ambo, from *ām*, a mango; Kesharbai, from *keshar*, saffron; and Lavengi, from *laveng*, cloves.

The availability of local products has created patterns in the evolution of Indian sweets so that those from Western and Southern India, for example, feature the various coconut products. Here, the coconut fruit itself is considered particularly auspicious. In the wheat-growing areas of the north, there are more dishes made with flour and wheat products such as semolina. Here, sweet breads, pancakes and pastries will be found. Climate and local custom provide further subtle influences which have given such great variety and interest to Indian sweet cookery. Not only sugar, fruits and vegetables have been pressed into service, but sometimes the very bark of trees and paper-thin sheets of beaten gold and silver, made edible by their thinness. A sweet may be quite plain and simple, though still exotic to the foreigner, or it may be exquisite in its beauty of form and presentation, its fleeting aroma and taste. But whatever form it may take, it will still be nourishing and however demanding it may have been in the making, the result will be a joy and delight both to the cook and those who partake of it. By using this book you will certainly enjoy creating food for the gods!

The Cook's Story

It is difficult for the blind to cook, though they may have a marvellous sense of smell and a highly developed sense of touch. It is possible, but more difficult than for those of us who are able to see. The celebrated cook, Deviprasad, remembered an experience as a boy which left a lasting impression on his memory. In those days his master, who was very strict but kind and compassionate also, used to give a feast once a year for some of the blind beggars of the town. At one of these feasts, when the beggars arrived a cripple was among them who obviously could see perfectly well. After making namaste to the master, the beggars seated themselves on the floor around the numerous dishes. The young Deviprasad noticed the cripple take a dish and quickly help himself to some of the tastiest food. He hobbled to a corner of the room where he could watch the rest.

'Watch them!' he called out to Deviprasad with a chuckle. 'They all think they know what they're eating. Just look at them though!' Deviprasad watched as the blind men reached out for the food. Soon they were sniffing and tasting and exchanging comments on the food.

'Oh! The master has made a special dish of rice,' said one.

'No he hasn't,' said another, 'this dish is lentils, not rice.' A third shouted, 'Rubbish! It's so obviously made from vermicelli, what is there to argue about?'

Then one furthest away from the quarrel said, 'Huh! All you can taste is something savoury. I assure you the food is sweet. I must have a superior sense of taste.'

'You see,' the cripple laughed as Deviprasad frowned, 'it's always the same. They always argue because they all think they're eating the same thing. Numbskulls, every one of them!'

Just then a hush came over the room. The beggars seemed to sense that a new presence had just entered. It was Deviprasad's master. 'That will do,' he said. 'You are all right. You are all eating the food that I have the honour of giving you. Each dish is different, but they all have one thing in common. We may begin where we wish. It may taste and smell and feel different to each one of us. But in the end we must all come to the same conclusion that we have eaten the Lord's food. Now let us enjoy it in peace together.'

Later his master spoke with Deviprasad. 'It is true. The beggars always argue amongst themselves. It gives them something to do, I think. When I prepare food I meditate on the divine aspect of life, present in all things. I know that some of those poor wretches do the same while they stumble about the town begging for alms. We may not be able to change our position very easily, but yet we all seek the same whether we are aware of it or not.'

Utensils and Serving

In this series of cookery manuals, the Indian way of looking at food has been stressed throughout. From this point of view, food possesses a divine nature and the act of eating is a divine necessity, an act of joy. Thus the cook prepares accordingly, bathing and purifying the body, the kitchen and the utensils to be used. The best possible ingredients are procured and where necessary these are carefully washed and made ready. The cook ensures that the mind is calm so that the work in hand may proceed in a joyful manner. This will greatly benefit both the cook and those who are going to partake of the food later on.

Heavy pans should be used wherever possible. Keep a separate non-stick pan for sweet things only. A concave iron dish (*tava*) for certain sweet breads may be purchased at many Asian stores, but a good frying-pan will do the job too. Wooden spoons are preferable to metal ones in some cases, and those used for sweet cooking should be kept for this kind of cooking only. A separate chopping board is best for nuts and sweet ingredients. Metal sieves and colanders will always come in handy. Try and acquire some nice ladles and little bowls since you will find them useful all the time. A pestle and mortar is a necessity. The most useful and cheapest to buy are made in India and cut from a light green or grey rock, left slightly roughened. These are now widely available in Asian stores. A good grinder could be used and a blender/liquidizer is a useful tool for the cook in a hurry.

Sweets and sweet dishes may form part of a meal, being eaten either before or after the main dishes, according to the taste of the diners. They make tasty, nourishing snacks at any time, especially for children, and they are ideally suitable for those on certain diets where a small amount of nutritious food is required. Those who practise the various forms of Yoga and meditation will also appreciate them. Finally, they are an excellent pick-me-up after strenuous exercise or illness.

Traditionally, sweets are served on polished metal trays (a large one is termed a *thāl* and the smaller individual one a *thāli*) or in separate metal bowls known as *katoris*. Drinks are sometimes served in stainless steel goblets. Any nice-looking dishes, plates, bowls and drinking vessels may be used, and decorations such as carefully chosen flowers and coloured napkins will add to the beauty of the presentation.

The Spices

In sweet cookery spices are used for their ability to perfume and aromatize the food as well as making a subtle contribution to the taste.

Gauri, the wife of Shiva, is worshipped during March or April by married women whose husbands are still alive. A brass swing (*dola*) containing the images of Shiva and his family is placed on a raised dais and worshipped every morning. A fresh wreath of flowers has to be added every day. During the whole period each family holds a meeting at which other women and girls are invited to attend. The image of Gauri is carefully dressed, and all the curiosities and interesting things in the house are arranged in front of the figures. Fruits, grains, sweets and flowers are then distributed amongst the visitors. The room is specially decorated and lit, and it is considered highly auspicious for newly married couples to be entertained there. This is a gala day for all women except widows, and the gathering is called the Turmeric and Saffron ceremony.

CARDAMOM (*elaichi*): This member of the ginger family is found in the high ranges of Kerala where tea is cultivated. These southern hills of Kerala have been named the Cardamom Hills because of the importance of the crop. It is a pungent aromatic, often chewed after eating as a digestive and breath-sweetener. It is sometimes used whole in the pods or the seeds removed and lightly crushed or ground.

CINNAMON (*dalchini*): The dried inner bark of cassia. Being an aromatic, it may be chewed to sweeten the breath and is said to strengthen the gums. True cinnamon (*Cinnamomum zeylanicum*) has a more delicate flavour than cassia and is not as pungent. This makes it more suitable, when available, for sweet dishes.

CLOVES (*lāung*): The dried fruit of *Myrtus caryophyllus* has always been the basis of the spice trade. Clove oil is antiseptic and strongly aromatic.

CUMIN (*jīra*): Used whole as seeds or ground, cumin is a member of the parsley family, like coriander.

FENNEL (*sānf*): These small, elongated, pale green seeds taste like aniseed or liquorice. They are one of the seeds handed round after a meal both as a digestive and as a breath-sweetener.

GINGER (*adrak*): Kerala is the main home of the ginger crop which has been cultivated there for thousands of years. The fresh root is always referred to in the recipes and powder should not be substituted. It is considered a health-giving digestive.

MINT (*podina*): The fresh leaves are used in a similar way to that of Western cooking, often as a garnish, especially in fresh drinks.

POPPY SEED (*khus khus*): These tiny creamy white or grey seeds stimulate the appetite. They thicken sauces and give a crunchy, pleasing texture to fillings. Only the seeds of the opium poppy (*Papaver somniferum*) are used.

SAFFRON (*kesha*): Perhaps the most expensive of all spices, it is the dried stigmata of the saffron crocus which have to be harvested by hand. It can colour many thousands of times its own weight of water and is usually soaked in warm water or milk to extract the brilliant yellow colour. It also has a fine, distinctive taste and aroma. Turmeric should never be used as a substitute.

SESAME SEED (*til*): Tiny, white, creamy or pale brown seeds giving a particularly nutty flavour. Sesame oil is a sweet oil used for cooking in some parts of the country. These highly nutritious seeds are associated with the worship of Lakshmi, the goddess of wealth and prosperity.

TAMARIND (*imali*): Usually purchased as a lump which consists of the seed pods and attached plant material. A piece should be broken off and soaked in warm water to extract its acidic watery pulp. It is used where its special tartness or piquancy is required.

Turmeric (*haldi*): The dried fleshy root of another member of the ginger family. It contains a bright yellow pigment and the robes of holy men are often dyed with it. To be used for this purpose, it must be made fast or the colour will run. Like chilli, it is an ingredient to be respected. Its warm and pungent flavour is very strong, and too much turmeric will overwhelm and ruin a dish. It can be used to colour rice when thrown into the boiling water after the rice.

Basic Ingredients

MILK: All good cow's milk is suitable for the recipes in this book. Where milk has to be boiled to become thick, high-fat milk such as Jersey will give a creamier taste and texture. Goat's milk may often be used but allowances should be made for a slight change in taste. Your own experiments are the best guide. In some cases condensed milk may save cooking time.

KHOYA: If fresh milk is boiled in a heavy pan for an hour or so, stirring to prevent sticking, a thick residue results. This khoya is the basis of many sweetmeats, though the cooking process is laborious. Khoya may be made from full-cream powdered milk by working 1½ tablespoons of hot water into every 2 tablespoons of milk powder to make 85 g (3 oz) of khoya. Baby milk with special additives is difficult to work with and will not be found to be a suitable substitute for simple full-cream powdered milk.

DAHI: Curd or yogurt is home-made by the country people. The dahi-seller deals in this commodity alone and makes it in enormous bowls. Plain, commercial yogurt is a handy substitute. To make 500 ml (2 pints) of yogurt you need 500 ml (2 pints) of milk and 3 heaped tablespoons of yogurt. Heat the milk until it almost boils. Pour it into a bowl and allow to cool until nearly lukewarm (the milk should still feel hot but not burn the skin). If the milk is too hot the culture grows faster and the curd is thicker and tougher. Gently stir in the yogurt which is at room temperature, cover the bowl and place on a warm blanket. Wrap the blanket round the bowl and leave to stand for at least five hours then put it in the refrigerator. Always keep half a cup of yogurt to use as a culture for the next batch. If your yogurt becomes too thin use some more fresh supply. A simple incubator can be made by fitting a small box with an electric bulb to give a temperature of

43° C and a place to store a bowl of curd. Once a routine is established, real yogurt can be enjoyed in the home every day.

CHENNA: Indian cottage cheese is made by putting dahi in a muslin bag and allowing it to drip overnight until the excess water is removed. If this cheese is pressed with a heavy weight till it hardens, the result is known as *panir*. Panir, like chenna, is an essential ingredient in certain sweetmeats.

GHEE: Ghee is clarified butter or margarine in which the water and any impurities have been driven off by heating. Good-quality ghee is available in tins, and vegetable ghee is also of excellent quality. If you want to make your own, place either butter or margarine in a pan and simmer for about an hour very gently. Strain and store in a jar or clean tin. Ghee is the traditional cooking medium of India from Vedic times when it was known as *ghrita* in Sanskrit. Butter may be substituted where ghee is indicated in the recipes. Corn, safflower or peanut oil may also be substituted when deep-frying.

SUGAR: Various forms of white sugar are usually used in making Indian sweets. This ensures that certain colours and flavours are not marred by the strong taste and colour of unrefined sugars or syrups. However, it is generally acknowledged today that the refined white sugar available in Europe and America contributes little or nothing towards health. In most of the recipes, brown, or unrefined sugar or honey can be used where healthy nourishment is the prime consideration. Unrefined Indian cane sugar is known as *gur* or *jaggery*. It has a pleasant individual taste and quality.

FLOUR, WHEAT, GRAM and RICE FLOUR: *Ata* is a whole-grain wheat flour which can only be bought in Asian grocers or health-food stores since it is not the wholemeal flour sold by Western bakers. When mixed with water it often takes on a distinctly sticky consistency.

When gram is ground the flour is known as *besan*. Many other members of the pea and bean family are made into a flour in India for use in pastry, batters and as ingredients in certain sweets. These flours will be popular with health-food enthusiasts since they contain the whole grain, and they have nothing added to them. They are also rich in protein.

Rice flour, ground rice, is used in sweets, pancakes and breads. It may often be substituted for the more lengthy process of grinding rice grains, but this substitution cannot be made where only coarse grinding is called for.

NUTS: Where nuts are included they should always be fresh and unsalted. Almonds should be blanched by boiling in a little water for a minute which makes them easy to peel. Where pistachios are used for decoration, as they frequently are, they should be chopped very finely and sprinkled like a powder for their best effect.

ROSEWATER: This is diluted essence of rose, now widely available in Asian, Middle Eastern and Greek stores. Only the best quality should be used. Thought to be introduced by the Mughals, its use is now popular throughout India.

COCONUT PRODUCTS: Coconut is used in Western- and Southern-style cooking. Make two holes in the natural depressions at the top of the coconut. Pour off the water. Tap round the middle of the shell with a hammer till it breaks in half. The white flesh can now be grated, chopped or squeezed. Coconut milk is made by extracting the juice from the white flesh. This process may be speeded up by adding a little hot water to the coconut flakes. It is always preferable to use fresh coconut, but creamed coconut is a great time-saver. You can buy this as a block which is cut up, and hot water added to make the coconut milk. Where grated coconut is called for in the recipe, for convenience, desiccated coconut from a packet may be used.

The coconut is considered as a highly auspicious offering. It is worshipped as the goddess Lakshmi in the absence of an image of her. When placed on top of the water jug it represents Varuna, the god of rain. This benevolent plant is the *Kalpa-vriksha*, or wish-granting tree, of ancient South Indian society. Its trunk supplies beams for cottages and serves as a boat when scooped out. The leaves provide roofing, the flowers yield a cooling drink, the fruit gives food and oil and a milk-like juice. The shell of the fruit gives medicinal oil and it can be made into small pots and ladles. Finally the husk supplies ropes and matting.

Weights and Measures

The simple weights and measures in the recipes are provided as a starting point for your own experimentation. They may be varied according to taste. The Indian housewife is used to guessing the amounts of the various ingredients, as is the male cook. More accurate measuring may be used when preparing larger quantities of food. Even then the cook will tend to judge by hand and sight according to the amount of raw materials available. In one family, two cooks using the same ingredients and same quantities will still produce different results and this is all part of the fascination.

Here is a comparison between Metric and Imperial systems:

approximately $\frac{1}{2}$ litre (500 ml) = approximately 18 fluid oz
approximately 30 grams = approximately 1 oz
approximately 450 grams = approximately 1 lb

The cup measurement in this book is one which holds 250 ml (8 fluid oz) of water, 250 g (8 oz) of sugar, 140 g (5 oz) of flour, 170 g (6 oz) rice.

A teaspoon holds approximately 5 ml ($\frac{1}{6}$ fluid oz), a dessertspoon approximately 15 ml ($\frac{1}{2}$ fluid oz) and a tablespoon approximately 30 ml (1 fluid oz), 30 g (1 oz) of ghee or sugar.

All measures are level ones. Though spoon and cup sizes vary, the intelligent cook will soon find out the amounts needed to obtain the desired results. You will find that the recipes are measured by container as well as weights and volumes to give practice in both systems of measurement.

In most cases the recipes are sufficient for 4–6 people.

The Gardener's Tale

Now one of the beggars present was sitting near to Deviprasad and his master and could not help but overhear their conversation. All at once he was plunged back to a certain warm evening when he was a boy, sitting at the feet of a kindly bearded man, a simple gardener. The boys had gathered, tired after the work of the day, because they felt relaxed and happy in his presence. It was said that he had once worked for a king. This man, who the beggar remembers as Krishnaprasad, would sit with the boys and serve them tea. Sometimes he would tell them stories to amuse them before they set out for their homes. The beggar could see himself as if it were yesterday, among the soft evening shadows. He saw himself as a boy turn to the gardener. The memory was so clear to him now that he decided to entertain the others by telling them how he recalled the scene.

'Sir,' began the boy, 'sometimes I become so tired with the hard work we have to do, I begin to wonder what is the use of it.' The old man smiled. 'Well, my son, do you want to grow up wise and a credit to your family or not?'

'Oh yes,' replied the boy, 'of course. But I wish it could happen by magic. I wish I already knew everything like you.'

Krishnaprasad chuckled, though he did not appear to be flattered. 'I know very little, sapling, and there is always something new to be learned every day. Sometimes we have to make mistakes in order to learn.'

'When mistakes are made, I always get the blame,' said the boy. 'I get fed up with it.'

'Naturally you would,' nodded Krishnaprasad. 'It is better not to blame at all but if blame must be given it should be given with justice.' Just then Krishnaprasad coughed and settled himself more comfortably. The boys knew that this was the sign for a story so they kept quiet and waited.

'You see, a nobleman was travelling to the palace of a king. In fact he was his country's ambassador to this king. He arrived towards dusk and found that a fine reception had been arranged in his honour. The king welcomed him to the city and showed the ambassador where he and his retinue could take their ease and refresh themselves after their long journey. In the evening, the ambassador was to be treated to a great banquet. However, the king was a little uneasy because he knew that the ambassador was renowned as a great connoisseur of food, especially sweet rice. Soon everyone had taken his place, and the wonderful dishes arrived. Then came the rice, a special recipe created by the king himself. But when he tasted it he knew at once that something must have gone wrong back in the kitchen. He glanced unhappily at his honoured guest and saw by the polite expression on the ambassador's face that his worst suspicions were well founded. Quietly he summoned a servant.

'"Ask the captain of the Royal Guard to come here immediately," he rasped. The captain arrived and bowed low. "Captain, I have been disgraced. Find out who prepared the rice for the banquet and deal with him so that it will never be carelessly done again!" The captain strode away and was soon in the kitchen quarters. The servants stepped back in alarm when they saw the grim look upon his face.

'"Who prepared the sweet rice?" he thundered.

'With his head hung low a young servant approached. "I did, sir."

'"Did you?" said the captain. "Well, just watch carefully all of you while I deal with the careless wretch who is to blame. It will ensure that such thoughtless behaviour will never occur again in this kitchen!" With that he took hold of the head cook and, drawing a heavy stick which he had been keeping behind his back, he gave the head cook a sound thrashing. At first the cook howled with pain, then took his punishment without a sound.

'Afterwards, the servants hurried to bathe his wounds and console the poor man. "Oh sir," said the young servant, "it was my fault. Why then did he beat you?"

'The cook somehow managed to smile at him. "You are wrong, my son. I am the one to blame, for it was I who taught you what to do. You see, there was a farmer who got kicked by a calf so he started to beat the cow, his poor mother. Now why should he do that? Well, the farmer reasoned to himself that the calf was born innocent, wasn't it? So where did he learn to kick? Only from his mother, so she gets the punishment!"'

One of Her thousand names is *Gudānnaprītamānāsa*, Fond of Sweetmeats.
(*Lalitāsahasranāman*)

Bonbons

One of the most popular and widely celebrated festivals is Divali, often called by its Sanskrit name Dipavali, meaning 'a row of lights'. It is celebrated on the last two days of the month of Asvin and the first two days of Kartik (October–November). In ancient times it was probably a fertility festival which later became associated with the coronation of Rama. Now the first day is dedicated to the goddess Lakshmi. Traders close their accounts on this day and begin new account books. On the fourth day earthen bowls filled with oil are lit in the evening and set up in rows outside the houses. To wish each other happy Divali, the people exchange greetings cards and gifts and it is a favourite day for giving sweets.

Sugared Almonds

500 g (1 lb) almonds, blanched and finely sliced
500 g (1 lb) icing sugar
rosewater
3 egg whites
1–2 tablespoons caster sugar
2 tablespoons pistachio nuts, finely chopped

Mix the almonds with the icing sugar, adding enough rosewater to make a thick paste. Spread the mixture evenly in a low tin which has been chilled or previously rinsed with cold water. Beat the egg whites till stiff and fold in the caster sugar. Spread over the almond paste and leave to set for about an hour. When nearly firm, sprinkle with pistachio nut, press in gently and cut into squares. This Persian recipe comes from the Punjab.

Frosted Cashewnuts

2 heaped tablespoons sugar
2 tablespoons milk
food colouring
5 heaped tablespoons cashewnuts

Mix the sugar and milk in a small pan, and add a dash of colouring to make a delicate colour. Heat gently until the mixture begins to thicken. Add the nuts and stir in well until the moisture is driven off. Turn out on to a dish and allow to cool. The nuts are frosted quite quickly and care must be taken not to overcook.

Jaggery Toffee (*Gur papedi*)

1 cup wholewheat flour (ata)
½ cup ghee
¼ cup grated coconut
¾ cup jaggery (gur)

Fry the flour in ghee until lightly brown. Add coconut and mix well. Melt the jaggery over a low heat, stir in and mix well. Pour into a dish and allow to cool. Cut in pieces when nearly set.

Nut Toffee

1 tablespoon pistachios
1 tablespoon almonds
1 tablespoon cashewnuts
½ tablespoon sesame seeds
170 g (6 oz) sugar
½ tablespoon ghee
1 teaspoon lemon juice
6 cardamoms, crushed seeds
1 dessertspoon rosewater

Lightly roast the nuts and sesame seeds, and grind or finely chop the nuts. Boil sugar with a dessertspoon of water and the ghee to form a thick syrup. Add lemon juice, nuts and sesame seeds, cardamom and rosewater. Mix well and quickly pour into a greased tray. Flatten and cut in pieces. Keep in an airtight container.

Coconut Toffee

½ cup brown sugar
½ cup water
½ grated coconut or 1 cup desiccated coconut
vanilla essence

Melt the sugar in water and boil till the scum appears. Skim off and add the coconut. Continue cooking on low heat for five minutes, stirring all the time. Add a few drops vanilla and keep stirring until the mixture thickens and begins to leave the sides of the pan. Turn on to a greased plate or dish. Allow to cool and cut in pieces. In Maharashtra this toffee or *vadi* is made in the same way with khoya and nuts. Add four tablespoons khoya and a tablespoon of sliced nuts to the ingredients and cook in the same way. Store in an airtight container.

Sesame Toffee

6 tablespoons sesame seeds
2 tablespoons peanuts
1 cup brown sugar
10 cardamoms, skinned and powdered
2 tablespoons grated coconut

Roast the sesame seeds gently till light brown. Allow to cool. Do the same with the peanuts and grind together. Add two cups of water to the sugar and boil to make a syrup of one-thread consistency. Add the ground nuts and seeds and cardamom powder, and stir until the mixture thickens and leaves the sides of the pan. Turn out on to a greased dish, flatten and sprinkle with the grated coconut. Mark the toffee before it sets to make cutting easier. Store in an airtight container.

Curd Toffee

500 g (1 lb) yogurt (curd)
500 g (1 lb) sugar
1 heaped tablespoon almonds, blanched and sliced
1 heaped tablespoon cashewnuts, sliced
pinch saffron, dissolved in 2 teaspoons milk
1 tablespoon pistachios
10 cardamoms, skinned

Hang the curd in a muslin cloth or bag and allow to drip overnight. Next day gently heat the thickened curd in a pan with the sugar and sliced nuts. Stir continuously until the mixture turns thick and leaves the sides of the pan. Stir in the saffron essence and mix well. Turn out on to a greased dish and flatten. Grind the pistachios and cardamom seeds and sprinkle over the toffee. Leave to cool. Store in an airtight container.

Peach Toffee

500 g (1 lb) fresh stoned or tinned peaches
500 g (1 lb) sugar
1 tablespoon almonds, blanched and sliced
10 cardamoms, skinned and powdered

Heat the fruit gently in a pan until it begins to thicken. Stir in the rest of the ingredients and continue stirring until the mixture turns thick and begins to leave the sides of the pan. Add a tablespoon of ghee. Stir in well and turn the mixture out on to a greased dish. Flatten and allow to cool. When cut store in an airtight container.

Tomato Toffee

500 g (1 lb) tomatoes
500 g (1 lb) sugar
1 cup grated coconut
1 tablespoon ghee
10 cardamoms, skinned and powdered

Strain the tomatoes through a fine sieve to remove the pips. Put in a pan with the sugar and heat gently. Meanwhile gently fry the coconut until it turns golden. Mix in with the tomatoes and sugar and add the cardamom. Keep stirring until the mixture turns thick and leaves the sides of the pan. Turn out on to a greased dish. Cut and store in an airtight container.

Cashewnut Toffee

500 g (1 lb) cashewnuts
500 g (1 lb) sugar
milk
10 cardamoms, skinned and powdered
1 tablespoon pistachios, finely chopped

Grind the cashewnuts finely. Mix the sugar with a tablespoon or two of milk in a pan to melt it. Heat this mixture for a few minutes and then add the cashewnuts and cardamom. Stir continuously on a gentle heat until the mixture turns thick and leaves the sides of the pan. Turn out on to a greased dish, flatten and sprinkle with the pistachios. Allow to cool, cut and store in an airtight container.

Semolina Toffee

1 cup semolina (suji)
1 cup grated coconut
2 tablespoons ghee
2 cups brown sugar
2 tablespoons milk
1 heaped tablespoon almonds, blanched and sliced
10 cardamoms, skinned and powdered
1 tablespoon pistachios, finely chopped

Fry the semolina and coconut in ghee until golden. Dissolve the sugar in a pan and heat gently for a few minutes. Add the semolina and coconut and almonds. Stir continuously until the mixture thickens. Stir in the cardamom. When the mixture leaves the sides of the pan, turn out on to a greased dish and sprinkle with the finely chopped pistachios. Allow to cool, cut and store in an airtight container.

Potato Toffee

2 cups brown sugar
2 tablespoons milk
2 cups mashed boiled potato
1 tablespoon ghee
1 tablespoon cashewnuts, sliced
1 tablespoon pistachios

Put the sugar and milk in a pan, and heat gently. Meanwhile gently fry the potato in ghee until lightly golden. Stir into the sugar and milk. Add the nuts and continue stirring until the mixture thickens and leaves the sides of the pan. Turn out on to a greased dish and sprinkle with ground or finely chopped pistachios. A pinch of powdered cardamom seeds may be added to the garnish also. Allow to cool, cut and store in an airtight container.

Marzipan Dates

whole fresh dates
almonds, blanched
powdered cardamom seeds
marzipan

Slit the dates and remove the stones. Put an almond in each date with a sprinkling of cardamom powder. Close up and cover with a thin envelope of marzipan.

Mesu

1½ cups sugar
¾ cup water
600 g (1¼ lb) ghee or unsalted margarine
1 heaped cup gram flour (besan)
1 tablespoon pistachios, finely chopped

Dissolve the sugar in water in a heavy pan on a low heat. Allow to thicken for a few minutes. In a separate pan melt the ghee or margarine and put a tablespoonful into the syrup. Now sieve the besan into the syrup, stirring carefully. From now on the process is continuous stirring to prevent burning while the melted ghee is added a tablespoonful at a time. Stir well after adding the ghee and add the next spoonful before the mixture becomes too thick. This is a good sweet for two people to make together, with one doing the stirring and the other adding the hot ghee. Eventually the mixture becomes quite thick and bubbles appear on the surface like tiny volcanoes. Now pour in the rest of the hot ghee, stirring vigorously. The mixture should fizz nicely which gives this sweet its characteristic aerated appearance. Turn out immediately on to a greased dish and flatten. Sprinkle on the pistachios and cut a diamond pattern on the sweet while it is still hot. Allow to cool, cut and store in an airtight container. Mesu is a difficult sweet to get right, but the effort is well worthwhile. It should be nicely aerated with a darker layer in the middle.

Fudges

Fudges often have the same consistency as the toffees in the previous recipes but they should not be allowed to become hard so that they are brittle when set.

Cheese Fudge *(Sandesh)*

2 cups panir or cottage cheese
yogurt
1 tablespoon pistachios, ground
6 cardamoms, skinned and powdered

See under Basic Ingredients for information on *chenna* and *panir*. Knead the cheese with a little yogurt to make a soft dough. Spread the dough on a lightly buttered hot plate or heavy pan and steam or very gently heat. When the dough hardens, sprinkle on the pistachio and cardamom. Cut in diamond shapes to serve.

Saffron Cheese Fudge *(Kasturi sandesh)*

500 g (1 lb) chenna or cottage cheese
110 g (¼ lb) sugar
good pinch saffron
1 dessertspoon milk
1 heaped tablespoon almonds, blanched
1 heaped tablespoon cashewnuts
1 tablespoon pistachios, ground

See *chenna* under Basic Ingredients. Mix the chenna well with the sugar. Dissolve the saffron in warm milk and mix into the chenna so that a nice yellow colour is made. Mix in the almonds and cashewnuts after grinding them coarsely, and gently heat the mixture in a heavy pan till it turns thick. Turn out on to a greased dish and sprinkle with the pistachios. This recipe comes from Bengal, where sweets made from chenna are very popular. On festive occasions, sandeshes are covered with thin sheets of gold or silver foil before being cut to serve. Allow to cool.

Orange Sandesh

1 orange
110 g (¼ lb) sugar
500 g (1 lb) chenna or cottage cheese

Squeeze the orange and mix the juice with the sugar. Stir into the chenna and gently heat in a heavy pan till the mixture thickens. (See *chenna* under Basic Ingredients.) Turn out on to a greased dish and allow to cool. A few drops of orange colour may be added if desired. This recipe can be used with other fruits instead of orange.

Coconut Sandesh

500 g (1 lb) chenna or cottage cheese
110 g (¼ lb) sugar
½ cup grated coconut
10 cardamoms, skinned and powdered

Mix the chenna well with the sugar. (See *chenna* under Basic Ingredients.) Add the coconut and heat gently in a pan until the mixture thickens. Add the cardamom and stir continuously until the thick mixture leaves the sides of the pan. Turn out on to a greased dish, allow to cool.

Almond Sandesh

500 g (1 lb) chenna or cottage cheese
110 g (¼ lb) sugar
110 g (¼ lb) ground almonds
1 tablespoon almonds, blanched and halved

Mix the chenna well with the sugar. (See *chenna* under Basic Ingredients.) Add the ground almonds and heat gently in a pan, stirring continuously until the mixture thickens and leaves the sides of the pan. Turn out on to a greased dish, flatten and decorate with the halved almonds. Allow to cool.

Plain Barfi

The barfi are traditionally prepared with khoya (dried fresh full-cream milk) as the basis. (See *khoya* under Basic Ingredients.)

225 g (8 oz) sugar
1 cup water
170 g (6 oz) dried full-cream milk
8 cardamoms, skinned and crushed
1 tablespoon pistachios, ground

Make a syrup by boiling sugar and water briskly. The syrup is ready when a drop forms a ball when put on the edge of a cold dish. Add the milk powder and cardamom. Mix well and if nice and thick, turn out on to a greased dish and allow to cool. Sprinkle with the pistachios to garnish.

Pistachio Barfi

60 g (2 oz) sugar
2 tablespoons water
110 g (4 oz) pistachios, ground
110 g (4 oz) khoya
green colouring (optional)

Make a syrup by boiling the sugar and water briskly to one-thread consistency. Stir in the pistachios and khoya, and heat gently until a thick dry mixture is obtained. Turn out on to a greased dish and allow to cool. Green colouring may be added with the khoya; make sure that this is well mixed in.

Cashewnut Barfi

60 g (2 oz) sugar
2 tablespoons water
110 g (4 oz) cashewnuts, ground
110 g (4 oz) khoya
1 dessertspoon rosewater
1 tablespoon pistachios, ground

Make a syrup by boiling the sugar and water briskly to one-thread consistency. Stir in the cashewnuts, khoya and rosewater, and heat gently until a thick dry mixture is obtained. Turn out on to a greased dish, sprinkle with the pistachios and allow to cool. The last two barfis are from Gujerat.

Coconut Barfi

85 g (3 oz) sugar
2 tablespoons rosewater
170 g (6 oz) grated coconut
85 g (3 oz) khoya
8 cardamoms, skinned and powdered
yellow or red colouring

Make a syrup by boiling the sugar with the rosewater. Stir in the coconut, khoya and cardamom with a few drops of colouring, and heat gently until the mixture thickens and becomes dry. Turn out on to a greased dish and allow to cool. This barfi is from Orissa.

Potato Barfi

85 g (3 oz) sugar
2 tablespoons rosewater
170 g (6 oz) potato, boiled, peeled and mashed
85 g (3 oz) khoya
1 tablespoon pistachios, ground

Make a syrup by boiling the sugar with the rosewater. Stir in the potato, khoya and pistachios, and heat gently until the mixture thickens and becomes dry. Turn out on to a greased dish and allow to cool. Further ground or finely chopped pistachios may be sprinkled over as a decoration.

Ginger Barfi

110 g (4 oz) fresh ginger, peeled
110 g (4 oz) sugar
60 g (2 oz) khoya
6 cardamoms, skinned and powdered

Crush the ginger in a pan with the sugar and heat gently to make a thick syrup. Stir in the khoya and cardamom, and continue stirring until the mixture is thick and dry. Turn out on to a greased dish.

Green Gram Barfi (*Mūng dāl barfi*)

1 cup mung dal
1 tablespoon ghee
1 cup full-cream milk powder
1 cup sugar
1 tablespoon almonds, blanched and sliced
10 cardamoms, skinned and powdered
1 tablespoon pistachios, ground

Wash the dal in water and leave to soak for a few hours. Drain and grind to a paste. Heat the ghee and gently fry the dal with the milk powder, mixing well. Meanwhile make a syrup by boiling the sugar with two tablespoons of water. Add the dal and khoya mixture, almonds and cardamom, and stir well. Continue heating gently until a thick dry mixture is formed. Turn out on to a greased dish, flatten and decorate with the pistachios. Allow to cool. This barfi is from Bengal.

Semolina Barfi

2 tablespoons ghee
1 cup semolina
1 cup grated coconut
½ cup brown sugar
½ cup milk powder
pinch saffron, dissolved in ½ cup warm milk
1 tablespoon cashewnuts, finely chopped
1 tablespoon almonds, blanched and sliced

Heat the ghee in a pan, and lightly fry the semolina and coconut. Add the sugar and milk powder with the saffron dissolved in half a cup of warm milk and the nuts. Continue stirring on a gentle heat until the mixture thickens and leaves the sides of the pan. Turn out on to a greased dish and allow to cool.

Pumpkin Barfi

- 1 kilo (2 lb) white pumpkin or marrow
- ½ cup milk
- 225 g (½ lb) sugar
- 225 g (½ lb) khoya
- 1 tablespoon almonds, blanched and sliced
- 1 tablespoon cashewnuts, chopped
- 1 teaspoon ghee

Peel the pumpkin or marrow and cut in very small pieces. Cook in the milk until tender. Mash well and add the rest of the ingredients, stirring on a gentle heat. Continue stirring until the mixture becomes thick and leaves the sides of the pan. Turn out on to a greased dish and allow to cool.

Gram Flour Barfi (*Besan barfi*)

- 225 g (½ lb) sugar
- 3 tablespoons ghee
- 500 g (1 lb) gram flour
- 225 g (½ lb) khoya
- 1 tablespoon almonds, blanched and sliced
- 1 tablespoon cashewnuts, chopped
- 10 cardamoms, skinned and powdered
- 1 tablespoon pistachios, ground

Make a syrup by boiling the sugar with half a cup of water. Meanwhile heat the ghee in another pan, and lightly fry the gram flour until it turns golden. Stir into the syrup with the khoya, nuts and cardamom. Heat gently and stir well until the mixture thickens and leaves the sides of the pan. Turn out on to a greased dish, flatten and sprinkle on the pistachio. Allow to cool. This recipe is from Gujerat.

Mysore Pak

3 tablespoons ghee
2 cups gram flour
1 cup sugar
1 tablespoon almonds, blanched and sliced
1 tablespoon cashewnuts, chopped
1 tablespoon sultanas
pinch saffron, dissolved in milk

Heat the ghee, and lightly fry the besan or black gram flour until golden. Make a syrup by boiling the sugar briskly with half a cup of water. Add to the fried flour and put in the nuts and sultanas. Dissolve the saffron in a dessertspoon of warm milk and stir into the mixture. Stir continuously on a low heat until the mixture thickens and leaves the sides of the pan. Turn out on to a greased dish and allow to cool. Pak, like the other fudges, can also be made into balls or flat cakes by rolling up the cooked mixture while it is still warm. This recipe is from South India.

Almond Pak

110 g (4 oz) sugar
110 g (4 oz) ground almonds
225 g (8 oz) khoya
1 dessertspoon rosewater
ghee

Make a syrup by boiling the sugar with two tablespoons of water. Stir in the almonds, and when a thick mixture is formed add the khoya and rosewater. Cook on a low heat, stirring continuously. Add a spoonful of melted ghee and continue stirring. Add a few more spoonfuls until the ghee cannot be absorbed by the sweet. Turn out on to a dish and leave to cool.

Milk Vadi

1 cup milk
1 cup sugar
1 cup full-cream milk powder
1 cup coconut milk or equivalent creamed coconut
2 tablespoons ground almonds
1 tablespoon cashewnuts, ground
6 cardamoms, skinned and powdered
1 dessertspoon rosewater
1 tablespoon pistachios, ground

Mix the milk and sugar in a pan, and gently heat until the sugar is dissolved. Stir in the milk powder, coconut milk and ground nuts. When the mixture starts to thicken, add the cardamom and rosewater. Keep stirring on a gentle heat until the mixture leaves the sides of the pan. Turn out on to a greased dish, flatten and sprinkle on the pistachios. Allow to cool.

Beveca

1 cup sugar
1 cup coconut milk or equivalent creamed coconut
2 tablespoons rice flour
1 tablespoon rosewater

Make a syrup by boiling the sugar with two tablespoons of water. Stir in the coconut milk and rice flour, and cook on a gentle heat until the mixture thickens, stirring continuously. Add the rosewater. Put the mixture in a greased baking dish and bake in a moderate oven until golden. This recipe is from Western India. In the Deccan Beveca is made with the following recipe. (In South India the semolina would be replaced with rice flour.)

250 g (½ lb) semolina
1 cup coconut milk or creamed coconut
4 eggs, beaten
3 tablespoons almonds, blanched
2 tablespoons ghee
½ teaspoon caraway seed
salt
brown sugar

Mix the semolina with the coconut milk and leave to soak for an hour. Meanwhile beat the eggs and grind the almonds to a paste. Add the eggs, almond paste, ghee, caraway seed, pinch of salt and sugar to taste to the semolina. Heat gently and stir until the mixture begins to thicken. Turn into a greased baking dish and bake in a moderate oven until golden.

Beveca can be cut up when cool and eaten as a fudge or left in its cake-like or pudding form and eaten as a dessert.

Cashewnut Fudge

110 g (4 oz) sugar
½ litre (1 pint) milk
110 g (4 oz) cashewnuts, ground
1 teaspoon rosewater
ghee, melted

Melt the sugar in the milk over a gentle heat. Add the cashewnuts and stir continuously until the mixture turns thick. Stir in the rosewater. Now add ghee by the spoonful, stirring all the time until the sweet will not absorb any more ghee. Turn out on to a dish, flatten and allow to cool. This recipe is from South India.

Bengal Semolina Fudge

1½ cups sugar
2 tablespoons ghee
1½ cups semolina
1 tablespoon almonds, blanched and sliced
1 tablespoon cashewnuts, chopped
4 cardamoms, skinned and powdered
pinch saffron, dissolved in milk
½ tablespoon pistachios, ground

Make a syrup by boiling the sugar with half a cup of water to one-thread consistency. Meanwhile heat the ghee and gently fry the semolina until golden. Stir into the syrup with the nuts, cardamom powder and saffron dissolved in a little warm milk. Stir the mixture continuously on a low heat until it turns thick and leaves the sides of the pan. Turn out on to a greased dish, flatten and sprinkle on the pistachios. Allow to cool. Yellow or orange colouring may be added but this will not be necessary if brown sugar is used.

Banana and Semolina Fudge

This is another semolina fudge with a typically South Indian flavour.

1½ cups semolina
2 tablespoons ghee
2–4 ripe bananas
½ cup grated jaggery or brown sugar
1½ cups coconut milk or creamed coconut
1 tablespoon almonds, blanched and sliced
4 cardamoms, skinned and powdered

Lightly fry the semolina in ghee until golden. Peel and mash the ripe bananas and mix in with the semolina. In a separate pan melt the jaggery or sugar with two tablespoons of water. Now add the semolina and bananas, coconut milk or creamed coconut, and stir continuously on a low heat until the mixture thickens and leaves the sides of the pan. Turn out on to a greased dish, flatten and sprinkle with the almonds and cardamom powder. Allow to cool.

Green Gram Fudge

1 cup green gram dal (mung dal)
1 cup yellow gram dal (channa dal)
1½ cups grated jaggery or brown sugar
ghee
1 cup grated coconut
pinch salt
8 cardamoms, skinned and powdered
1 tablespoon pistachios, ground

Soak the dals in water for a few hours to soften. Drain and grind to a paste. Meanwhile make a syrup by boiling the sugar with half a cup of water. Lightly fry the coconut in two tablespoons of ghee, then fry the dal paste until golden in a little more ghee. Stir into the syrup with the salt and cardamom powder, and cook gently until the mixture thickens and leaves the sides of the pan. Turn out on to a greased dish, flatten and sprinkle with the pistachios. Allow to cool. This fudge is known in South India as Ukkarai. Extra nuts and saffron essence may also be added for extra flavour.

Coconut Fudge

- 4 tablespoons ghee
- 1 cup wholewheat flour
- 1 cup grated coconut
- 1 cup jaggery or brown sugar
- ½ cup coconut milk or creamed coconut
- 1 tablespoon poppy seeds
- 8 cardamoms, skinned and powdered
- 1 teaspoon almonds, blanched and sliced
- 1 tablespoon pistachios, ground

Heat the ghee, and lightly fry the flour and coconut. Melt the sugar in coconut milk, and stir in the flour and coconut. Cook on a low heat, stirring continuously until the mixture thickens. Add the poppy seeds and cardamom powder. When the mixture leaves the sides of the pan, turn out on to a greased dish, flatten and sprinkle on the nuts. Allow to cool. This recipe is from Gujerat.

Halvas

Halvas are made by reducing vegetables or fruits with sugar. An essential part of the technique is to add spoonfuls of ghee to the thick mixture and to continue adding and stirring it in until the mixture will not absorb any more. The halva is then ready. The Halvai of Northern India are the caste and profession of confectioners.

Carrot

570 ml (1 pint) milk
1 kilo (2 lb) carrots, grated
140 g (5 oz) brown sugar
60 g (2 oz) creamed coconut or ghee
60 g (2 oz) ghee
15 cardamoms, skinned and powdered
18 almonds, blanched and sliced

Boil the milk and carrots gently until the mixture thickens, stirring continuously. Add the sugar and cook for a further fifteen minutes. Now add the creamed coconut and ghee, and cook gently until the mixture thickens. Add a few drops of colouring to make the halva a glowing colour. Stir in well, and keep adding spoonfuls of ghee and stirring until the thick lump will not absorb any more ghee. Turn out on to a greased dish, flatten and sprinkle with cardamom and sliced nuts. Allow to cool before cutting.

Banana

2 tablespoons ghee
4–6 ripe bananas
¾ cup sugar
6 cardamoms, skinned and powdered
1 tablespoon almonds, blanched and sliced

Heat the ghee and lightly fry the bananas. Mash well and add the sugar and cardamom powder. Cook gently until a lump is formed. Add spoonfuls of ghee until no more ghee is absorbed by the halva. Turn out on to a dish, flatten and sprinkle with the almonds. A little yellow colouring may be added while cooking the halva if desired.

Orange

2 oranges
1 cup sugar
3 tablespoons ghee
1 cup rice flour
1 teaspoon orange or saffron essence
1 tablespoon pistachios, ground

Cut the oranges in half and squeeze out the juice. Finely grate the peel. Meanwhile make a syrup by boiling the sugar with the orange juice. Heat the ghee and lightly fry the rice flour with the grated orange peel. Add the syrup and essence, and continue stirring on a low heat until the mixture becomes thick and the ghee begins to separate from the lump. Turn out on to a dish, flatten and sprinkle with pistachios. Cut when cool.

Marrow

Peel and grate the marrow and cook in the same way as for Carrot Halva. A tablespoon of fried sultanas makes a nice addition to the flavour.

Potato

½ kilo (1 lb) potatoes
300 g (10 oz) sugar
pinch saffron, dissolved in milk
4 cardamoms, skinned and powdered
110 g (4 oz) khoya
ghee
1 tablespoon almonds, blanched and sliced

Boil the potatoes, peel and mash. Add the sugar to the potatoes in the pan. Cook on a low heat until most of the water is driven off. Add the saffron dissolved in a little milk, cardamom powder, khoya and a tablespoon of ghee. Stir continuously until the mixture thickens. Add teaspoons of ghee, stirring them in until the lump will not absorb any more. Turn out on to a dish, flatten and sprinkle with the sliced nuts. Cut when cool.

Green Gram

1 cup green gram (mung dal)
2 tablespoons ghee
1 cup sugar
1 tablespoon sultanas, fried in ghee
1 cup milk
6 cardamoms, skinned and powdered
pinch saffron, dissolved in milk
1 tablespoon almonds, blanched and sliced

Soak the dal for a few hours to soften. Drain and grind to a paste. Lightly fry the paste in ghee until golden. Add the sugar, sultanas and milk and cook on a low heat, stirring continuously. When the mixture thickens, add the cardamom and saffron dissolved in a little milk. When the mixture forms a lump, add more ghee if necessary until the lump will not absorb any more. Turn out on to a dish, flatten and sprinkle on the almonds.

Gram

1 cup gram dal
1½ cups grated coconut
1½ cups sugar

Wash and boil the dal until soft. Add the coconut and sugar, and continue cooking on a low heat until the mixture thickens. Add two tablespoons of ghee and cook, stirring continuously until a lump is formed and the ghee separates out. Turn out on to a dish. Cut when cool. This simple halva is good for invalids or those needing a quick pick-me-up snack.

Peanut

700 g (1½ lb) peanuts
4 tablespoons ghee
225 g (½ lb) sugar
1 tablespoon raisins or sultanas, fried in ghee
6 cardamoms, skinned and powdered
pinch saffron, dissolved in milk
1 tablespoon pistachios, ground

Soak the uncooked peanuts for an hour. Drain and grind to a paste. Heat the ghee and fry the paste gently until it is lightly golden. Add the sugar, sultanas, cardamom powder and saffron dissolved in a little milk. Cook gently on a low heat, stirring continuously until the mixture thickens. Now add spoonfuls of ghee, and continue stirring and mixing until the lump will not absorb any more ghee. Turn out on to a dish, flatten and sprinkle on the pistachios. Cut when cool.

Cashewnut

350 g (12 oz) cashewnuts
1 cup grated coconut
2 tablespoons ghee
3 cups sugar
4 cardamoms, skinned and powdered

Soak the nuts in water for an hour, drain and grind to a paste. Lightly fry the paste and coconut in ghee until golden. Add the sugar and a cup of water, and cook the mixture until the halva forms a lump. Add a tablespoon of ghee. Stir in and turn out on to a greased dish. Flatten and sprinkle on the cardamom powder. Cut when cool.

Beetroot

- ½ kilo (1 lb) beetroot
- 1 cup sugar
- 4 tablespoons ghee
- 1 tablespoon cashewnuts, chopped
- 1 tablespoon sultanas, fried in ghee
- 6 cardamoms, skinned and powdered
- 1 tablespoon almonds, blanched and sliced

Peel the beetroots and slice well. Put in a pan with a little water and cook till tender. Using pre-cooked beetroots will save some of this cooking time. Drain and mash. Add the sugar and cook over a low heat until the mixture begins to thicken. Stir in the cashewnuts, sultanas and cardamom powder along with the ghee, and keep stirring until the mixture forms a lump and the ghee separates out. Turn out on to a dish, flatten and press on the almonds. Cut when cool.

Semolina

- 4 tablespoons ghee
- 1 tablespoon sultanas
- 1 cup semolina
- 4 cardamoms, skinned and powdered
- 1 cup sugar
- 4 cloves
- small piece cinnamon
- 1 tablespoon almonds, blanched and sliced
- 1 tablespoon rosewater
- 1 tablespoon pistachios, ground

Heat the ghee and fry the sultanas and semolina until golden, stirring continuously. Add the cardamom, sugar, cloves, cinnamon and 2 cups of water. Cook on a low heat until the mixture thickens. Add the almonds and rosewater, and continue cooking until a lump is formed and the ghee separates out. Turn out on to a greased dish, flatten and sprinkle on the pistachios. Serve hot or cold with cream.

Rice Flour

- 1½ cups grated jaggery or brown sugar
- 2 cups coconut milk or creamed coconut
- 1 cup rice flour
- 1 tablespoon cashewnuts, chopped
- 6 cardamoms, skinned and powdered
- ghee

Put the sugar and coconut milk in a pan and warm gently. When the sugar has dissolved, add the rice flour and continue stirring until the mixture thickens. Add the nuts and cardamom and a tablespoon of melted ghee. Keep stirring and adding ghee until a lump is formed and no more ghee is absorbed by the halva. Turn out on to a dish, flatten and allow to cool. The halva may be decorated with ground nuts or coconut as it sometimes is in South India.

Semolina and Coconut

1 cup sugar
4 tablespoons ghee
1 cup semolina
3 tablespoons grated coconut
1 tablespoon almonds, blanched and sliced
4 cardamoms, skinned and powdered
1 tablespoon pistachios, ground

Make a syrup by boiling the sugar with a cup of water. Meanwhile heat the ghee and lightly fry the semolina until golden. Add the syrup, coconut, almonds and cardamom, and cook on a low heat until a lump is formed, stirring continuously. Add spoonfuls of ghee and keep stirring until no more ghee is absorbed by the halva. Turn out on to a dish, flatten and sprinkle on the pistachios. Cut when cool.

Bombay Halva

1 cup sugar
pinch saffron, dissolved in milk
2 cups water
3 tablespoons ghee
¾ cup semolina
2 tablespoons sultanas
4 cardamoms, skinned and powdered
1 tablespoon almonds, blanched and sliced

Mix the sugar with the saffron dissolved in 2 tablespoons warm milk. Add the water and boil gently to make a syrup. Meanwhile heat the ghee and gently fry the semolina until golden. Add the sultanas. Pour in the syrup and cook on a low heat until the mixture forms a lump. Add another tablespoon of ghee and stir in. Turn the halva out on to a dish, flatten and sprinkle on the cardamom and nuts. Serve hot or cold.

This halva can also be prepared with wholewheat flour (ata) or gram flour (besan). It is often served in the north with puris.

Karachi Halva

This halva is somewhat like the well-known sweet Turkish Delight.

550 g (1¼ lb) sugar
½ litre (1 pint) water
110 g (4 oz) cornflour
a few drops yellow colouring
2 teaspoons lemon juice
ghee
1 tablespoon rosewater
1 tablespoon almonds, blanched and sliced
10 cardamoms, skinned and powdered
1 tablespoon pistachios, ground

Make a syrup by boiling the sugar with water. Mix the cornflour with a cup of water, making sure there are no lumps. Stir into the syrup. Cook on a low heat, stirring continuously. Add the colouring and lemon juice. When the mixture thickens add a spoonful of ghee, the rosewater, almonds and cardamom. Keep stirring and adding ghee until a lump is formed which will no longer absorb any ghee. Turn out on to a dish, flatten and sprinkle on the pistachios. Cut when cool.

Madras Halva

½ kilo (1 lb) sugar
2 cups water
225 g (8 oz) semolina
1 tablespoon poppy seeds
4 tablespoons grated coconut
8 cardamoms, skinned and powdered
ghee

Make a syrup by boiling the sugar and water. Meanwhile lightly roast the semolina, poppy seeds and coconut in a pan on a gentle heat. Stir into the syrup and cook until the mixture thickens. Stir in the cardamom. Continue cooking, adding spoonfuls of ghee, until a lump is formed which will not absorb any more ghee. Turn out on to a dish and cut when cool.

Halva Sohan

½ kilo (1 lb) sugar
1 cup water
½ cup coconut milk or creamed coconut
110 g (4 oz) rice flour
a few drops red colouring
1 tablespoon rosewater
1 tablespoon almonds, blanched and sliced
ghee
1 tablespoon pistachios, ground

Make a syrup by boiling the sugar with water. Stir in the coconut milk and boil gently for a further five minutes. Stir in the rice flour and red colouring, and cook on a low heat until the mixture thickens. Add the rosewater and almonds and a tablespoon of melted ghee. Keep stirring and adding spoonfuls of ghee until a lump is formed which will not absorb any more. Turn out on to a dish, flatten and sprinkle on the pistachios. Cut when cool.

The Ambassador's Tale

'But the ambassador was a good-hearted man,' the gardener continued, 'and a man used to speaking his mind. He felt that it would bode well for his mission if he could save the king some embarrassment. After the banquet, when he and the king sat together, he thanked the king for his hospitality. "Your table is wonderful, your majesty, in spite of the fact that I hear your best cook is unwell. It would be a great honour for me if you would allow me to lend you my own cook until yours recovers his health once more."

'The king was pleasantly surprised. "How kind, your excellency. Yes, it is true that my best cook is not at all well and I fear the food would not be as well prepared as you are accustomed to. But to surrender your own esteemed cook would indeed be a sacrifice I could not match."

' "Not at all, your majesty. But hardly what I would call a sacrifice. I have heard a story in your country which to me tells of true sacrifice."

'"Please tell me this story," said the king.

'"Well," the ambassador continued, "the story says that after a great battle, a lord and his brothers were celebrating the victory with a sumptuous ceremony. Many gifts of money and jewels were given to the people by these rich brothers, and everyone was commenting on the great sacrifice that they were making thereby. But just then the appearance of an unusual-looking mongoose, whose body was half golden and shining brightly, brought a hush to the gathering. He addressed the crowd saying that he did not consider that any sacrifice was being made. The crowd was aghast at this, but all the same intrigued by the strange animal who was able to talk.

'"These rich men can afford to give such gifts," cried the mongoose. "It is no sacrifice to them. In a little village far from here used to live a poor Brahmin and his wife, his son and his son's wife. Then came a time of terrible food shortage in his part of the country and the Brahmin could not earn enough to buy food. When the family were starving he came home one evening with a little flour given by a neighbour in exchange for some teaching. He divided the flour into four parts and his wife prepared to make the food for the family. Just as they were about to eat a guest called at the door. Because guests are treated as sacred visitors in India, the poor Brahmin welcomed him in and offered him his own portion of food.

'"I have been starving for days," the guest gasped, "have you any more?" At that, the wife offered him her share. Still the man's hunger was not appeased and he begged for more. So the son offered his share, saying that he must follow the example of his father. But the portions were so small that the guest said he still felt hungry. So the son's wife said she must behave according to the high principles of the family and she offered her share of food. At last the guest was satisfied and, after a little rest, he blessed the family and took his leave. That night, all living in the poor Brahmin's house died.

' "I had been looking for snakes and I was curled up in the corner watching this," said the mongoose. "When the last one had died, I ran over to the fire to see if I could find a scrap to eat for myself. Some of the flour had been spilt around the fire where the good wife had cooked the night before. As this flour touched my body it became golden wherever it fell, as you can see. Since that blessed moment I have travelled the country to try to find a sacrifice such as that poor family made so that I could turn the rest of myself to gold. But I have never found one. And I have not found one here. That is why I say to you all, this is no great sacrifice!"

'At this point, the ambassador turned to the king to see his reaction. There were tears in the king's eyes. "You are right," he said. "That was true sacrifice and such sacrifice is rare!"'

Sweets in Syrup

The earth is worshipped by farmers as a special manifestation of the Divine. During the month of Ashvin (September–October) sweetmeats are prepared at home and taken to the farm. There, five stones are gathered to form an altar. The sweets are then offered to the earth. After this, tiny portions are scattered over the farm. The family then gather for a celebratory meal.

Milk Crescents (*Khoya pantua*)

3 tablespoons wholewheat flour
12 cardamoms, skinned and powdered
350 g (12 oz) full-cream milk powder
2 cups sugar
1 tablespoon rosewater
ghee

Mix the flour, milk powder and cardamom in a bowl. Add enough water to make a smooth dough. Divide the dough into small balls and form each into a crescent shape. Make a syrup by boiling the sugar with a cup of water to one-thread consistency. Stir in the rosewater. Deep-fry the crescents until golden over a gentle heat. Dip in the syrup and serve hot or cold.

Cottage Cheese Crescents (*Chenna pantua*)

See *chenna* under Basic Ingredients. This recipe is like the previous one, but substitute half of the khoya with chenna or cottage cheese. If only chenna is used, less water will be necessary to make a dough.

Gram Crescents (*Dāl pantua*)

See *besan* under Basic Ingredients. Make up the crescents as in Milk Crescents, but use half khoya and half gram flour to make the dough. Plain flour or wholewheat flour is used to bind. Serve up in syrup as before.

Coconut Crescents (*Nareal pantua*)

2 cups grated coconut
2–3 tablespoons flour
12 cardamoms, skinned and powdered
2 cups sugar
1 tablespoon rosewater
ghee

Make a dough as in Milk Crescents, using the flour to bind. Stir the essence into the syrup and serve hot or cold.

Pantua comes from Bengal. They can be made from a variety of ingredients such as sweet potatoes or green bananas. Make up two cupfuls into a dough as in Coconut Crescents and serve in syrup.

Thick Milk Balls (*Gulāb jāmun*)

225 g (8 oz) full-cream powdered milk
1 tablespoon plain flour
1 tablespoon baking powder
milk
ghee for deep-frying
1 cup sugar
2 cups water
2 tablespoons rosewater

Sift together the milk powder, flour and baking powder. Add enough milk (10–12 tablespoons) to make a soft, stiff dough. Leave to stand for an hour. Form the dough into walnut-sized balls. Heat the ghee and gently deep-fry the balls until golden. The ghee should not be too hot, or the balls will only cook on the outside. Meanwhile make a syrup by boiling the sugar and water for a few minutes. Add the rosewater. Put the drained jamuns in the hot syrup and allow to soak before serving.

Nuts, cardamom seeds or small pieces of sugar candy can be inserted in the balls before cooking. Yogurt can be used to make the dough instead of milk, giving a tarter flavour. A nuttier consistency can be obtained by using 110 g (4 oz) ground almonds and 110 g (4 oz) plain flour instead of milk powder. Combine with the baking powder and rub in two tablespoons of ghee. Make up the dough with yogurt and cook as above. Gulab jamuns are a favourite Bengal sweet and also very popular throughout most of India. When the balls are given an elongated, plum-like shape they are known as jamuns.

Cheese Balls (*Kala jāmun*)

500 g (1 lb) panir
3 tablespoons sugar
2 tablespoons plain flour
2 tablespoons khoya
1 tablespoon baking powder
few drops red colouring
ghee for deep-frying
2 cups sugar
2 tablespoons rosewater

Beat the panir until smooth, and mix in 3 tablespoons sugar, the flour, khoya, baking powder and red colouring. Make up a smooth, stiff dough, adding a little milk if necessary. Leave to stand for an hour. Form the dough into walnut-sized balls and shape to make jamuns. Heat the ghee and gently deep-fry until golden. Meanwhile make a syrup by boiling the 2 cups sugar with 4 cups of water for a few minutes. Add the rosewater. Put the drained jamuns in the syrup and allow to soak. In Bengal these jamuns are taken out of the syrup the following day and served in pastry cases.

South Indian Sweet Potato Balls

250 g (½ lb) sweet potato, boiled, peeled and mashed
2 tablespoons cream or yogurt
2 tablespoons plain flour
½ cup coconut, grated
1 tablespoon ground almonds
6 cardamoms, skinned and powdered
ghee for deep-frying
1 cup sugar
2 cups water
1 tablespoon rosewater

Mix the potato, cream and flour to a smooth dough. Mix the coconut with the ground almonds and cardamom and divide into small portions. Form the dough around the coconut mixture to make jamuns. Heat the ghee and gently deep-fry the jamuns until golden. Meanwhile make a syrup by boiling the sugar and water for a few minutes. Add the rosewater and put in the drained jamuns to soak.

This recipe has a typically South Indian flavour. Other fillings could be invented and used in the same way.

Curd Balls (*Rasgullas*)

4 cups full-cream milk
juice of 2 lemons
1 tablespoon plain flour
1 cup sugar
2 cups water
1 tablespoon rosewater

Heat the milk to boiling-point and add the lemon juice. Leave to curdle. When the milk has curdled, pour into a muslin bag or cloth and allow the excess liquid to drain off. Press the bag with a weight and leave to drain again. Once the solid chenna has been formed, add the flour and knead to make a soft dough. Form into small balls. Meanwhile make a syrup by boiling the sugar with the water for a few minutes. Carefully put in the balls and cook gently in the syrup for fifteen minutes. Cool and sprinkle on the rosewater. Serve chilled in the syrup.

Curd and Nut Balls (*Rāj bhog*)

225 g (½ lb) panir
½ teaspoon powdered saffron
1 tablespoon semolina
1 teaspoon baking powder
1 tablespoon almonds, blanched and finely sliced
1 tablespoon pistachios, finely sliced
2 cups sugar
4 cups water
2 tablespoons rosewater

Make panir as in the previous recipe. (See also *panir* under Basic Ingredients.) Beat the saffron into the panir, and knead with the semolina and baking powder to make a smooth dough. If necessary add a little plain flour to help bind the dough, which should not be too sticky to handle. Form the dough into small balls around portions of the sliced nuts. Meanwhile make a syrup by boiling the sugar and water for a few minutes. Carefully put in the curd balls. Cover the pan and sprinkle the lid with cold water. Simmer very gently for ten minutes. The balls will now swell up. Take from the heat and sprinkle on the rosewater. Serve chilled.

Cheese Boats (*Cham cham*)

4 cups full-cream milk
juice of 2 lemons
1 tablespoon plain flour
few drops orange colouring
1 cup sugar
2 cups water
1 tablespoon rosewater

Make panir as in the recipe for Rasgullas. Knead with the flour and colouring to form an orange dough. Form into small balls and shape each ball into a little boat. Make up the syrup by boiling the sugar and water for a few minutes. Carefully put in the boats and cook gently for fifteen minutes. Once the boats puff up, leave to cool overnight. Next day sprinkle on the rosewater before serving. Serve chilled in the syrup.

Thick Milk and Cheese Boats (*Khoya cham cham*)

Make up the cham cham as in the previous recipe. Meanwhile make a garnish with the following:

1 cup khoya
pinch saffron, ground
1 tablespoon sugar
1 tablespoon pistachios, ground

Mix the khoya with the saffron until it turns bright yellow. (See *khoya* under Basic Ingredients.) Over a gentle heat stir together with the sugar to make a thick mixture. Take the cham chams from the syrup and spread with the khoya mixture. Finally sprinkle with the pistachios. They can be served with some of the chilled syrup. Like rasgullas, cham chams come from Bengal, the home of curd and curd-cheese sweets.

Flour Spirals (*Jalebi*)

1½ cups plain flour
2 tablespoons yogurt
1 teaspoon saffron or yellow colouring
2 cups sugar
2 cups water
ghee or oil for deep-frying

Sieve the flour into a basin, and add the curd and enough water (about a cup) to make a thick batter. Beat in the saffron or colouring and allow to stand in a warm place overnight. Boil the sugar and water for ten minutes to make a thick syrup. Keep warm. Beat the batter again. Heat the ghee in a pan for deep-frying. Fill a small funnel, or coconut shell with a hole in it, with batter. Keep a finger over the hole and hold over the hot ghee. Remove the finger and allow the stream of batter to make a spiral shape a little bigger than a cup in diameter. Fry until golden on both sides, remove and drain and allow to soak in the syrup. Remove the jalebis and pile them in a dish. Serve hot or cold.

For an alternative type of batter, mix a cup of wholewheat flour (ata) with half a cup of gram flour (besan) or black gram flour (urhad dal) and make up the batter in the usual way.

Jalebi Pudding

jalebis
2 cups milk
small piece cinnamon or lemon peel
6 eggs
1 tablespoon sugar
12 almonds, blanched and sliced

First make a custard. Boil the milk with the cinnamon stick or lemon peel. Remove and allow to cool. Beat the yolks of the eggs and keep the whites separate. Pour in the cold boiled milk, sugar and almonds. Beat the egg-whites to a stiff froth and stir in. Now arrange the jalebis, made as in the previous recipe, in an oven-proof bowl or dish and pour over the custard mixture. Bake in a moderate oven until firm. Serve hot or cold. Jalebi pudding is an excellent dish for children and for those who are recovering from illness.

Bundi

Make a batter as for jalebis. Pass through a sieve with large holes into the hot ghee. Remove the fried balls and put in thick syrup. In Bengal the batter is sometimes made with equal portions of semolina and rice flour. Sprinkle the syrup with a tablespoon of rosewater, a tablespoon of ground pistachios and six cardamoms, skinned and powdered.

Stuffed Sweet Potato Balls (*Rangālū pithe*)

½ kilo (1 lb) sweet potatoes, boiled, peeled and mashed
2 tablespoons flour
1 cup grated coconut
2 tablespoons brown sugar
8 cardamoms, skinned and powdered
milk
2 cups sugar
4 cups water

Knead the sweet potato and flour and leave aside. Mix the coconut, sugar and cardamom in a pan with enough milk to just dissolve the sugar (2–3 tablespoons). Cook over a gentle heat until a thick mixture is formed. Make a syrup by boiling the 2 cups of sugar with the water. Divide the potato dough into small balls, make a hole in each and put in a portion of the coconut filling mixture. Roll up again with the help of a dusting of flour. Deep-fry the pithe until golden, over a gentle heat. Drain and soak in the syrup. Serve hot or cold.

Stuffed Gram Balls (*Dāl pithe*)

½ kilo (1 lb) green gram (mung dal)
2–3 tablespoons flour
1 tablespoon pistachios, ground
filling as for Sweet Potato Balls
1 tablespoon rosewater

Wash the dal and leave to soak for a few hours. Cook in 2 cups of water until soft and dry. Add a little water during the cooking if necessary. Mash well and add enough flour to make a smooth dough. Mix in the pistachios and knead again. Make into small balls and fill with the filling mixture. Deep-fry in ghee until golden over a gentle heat. Make up a syrup with 2 cups of sugar as in the previous recipe and soak the pithe in the syrup. Sprinkle over the rosewater. Serve hot or cold.

Stuffed Rice Flour Balls (*Poli pithe*)

2 cups rice flour
2 cups hot water
1 cup grated coconut
2 tablespoons brown sugar
3 tablespoons khoya
8 cardamoms, skinned and powdered
milk
2 cups sugar
4 cups water

Put the rice flour in a pan with the hot water and cook on a low heat until the mixture forms a lump. Allow to cool. Mix the coconut, sugar, khoya and cardamom over a gentle heat with a little milk to form a thick mixture for the stuffing. Shape the rice flour into small balls with the aid of a little ghee on the hands. Fill with portions of the stuffing and steam for fifteen minutes until cooked. This can be done by putting the pithe in a cloth, in a colander over a pan of boiling water. Meanwhile make up the syrup and soak the steamed pithe in the syrup. Serve hot or cold.

Pithe come from Bengal. Various stuffings can be made up. Try adding sliced nuts and fried sultanas. The syrup may be flavoured with rosewater or saffron. This is where the ingenuity of the cook comes into play and cooking becomes experimental and fun.

Stuffed Black Gram Balls (*Ras vadas*)

1 cup urhad dal flour
1 cup khoya
1 tablespoon sultanas, fried and chopped
1 tablespoon almonds, blanched and sliced
2 cups sugar
4 cups water
ghee for deep-frying
1 tablespoon rosewater

Mix the flour and khoya to make a smooth dough, adding a little milk if necessary. Divide the dough into small balls and make a hole in each. Fill with a portion of sultana and nuts. Roll up and keep aside. Make a syrup by boiling the sugar and water. Deep-fry the balls in ghee over a gentle heat until golden. Put the drained balls in the syrup and sprinkle on the rosewater.

Fritters (*Mal poa*)

1 cup flour
1 teaspoon baking powder
yogurt
milk
ghee for deep-frying
1 cup sugar
2 cups water
pinch saffron dissolved in warm milk

Sift the flour and baking powder. Add enough yogurt to make a stiff paste. Now add a little milk to make a thick batter. Drop tablespoonfuls into the hot ghee and fry until golden. Remove and allow to drain. Make a syrup by boiling the sugar and water for a few minutes. Stir in the saffron dissolved in a little warm milk. Put in the fritters, allow to soak and serve hot with the syrup. They can be made a little more tasty by adding flavourings such as aniseed or cardamom to the flour when making the batter. In each case grind the spice. Rosewater could also be used to aromatize the syrup.

Rice and Semolina Puri

1 cup wholewheat flour
1 cup rice flour
2 tablespoons ghee
6 cardamoms, skinned and powdered
coconut milk or creamed coconut
ghee for deep-frying
2 cups sugar
4 cups water
2 tablespoons rosewater
grated coconut

Sift the flours together and rub in the two tablespoons of melted ghee. Work in the cardamom powder and knead to make a stiff dough, adding a little coconut milk, milk or water. Roll out to pastry thickness and cut out rounds the same diameter as a cup. Alternatively, make the dough into small balls and roll out each to make a puri. Deep-fry in hot ghee until golden. Make a syrup by boiling the sugar with the water for a few minutes. Stir in the rosewater. Dip the puris in the syrup until well soaked, roll in the coconut or some ground pistachios and serve hot.

Cheese Balls with Thick Milk Filling

Ingredients to make Rasgullas and syrup: see page 68

For the filling:
1 cup khoya
1 tablespoon brown sugar
1 tablespoon pistachios, ground

Make up the rasgullas and put in the syrup overnight. Next day mix the khoya with sugar. (See *khoya* under Basic Ingredients.) Drain the balls from the syrup and cut each in half. Spread a nice layer of khoya on one half and press on the other. Put all the filled balls on a dish. Any left-over khoya can be spread on the tops. Finally sprinkle the balls with the pistachios.

Flour Rolls (*Kalkals*)

1 cup flour
coconut milk or creamed coconut
ghee for deep-frying
2 cups sugar
2 cups water
8 cardamoms, skinned and powdered

Mix the flour with enough coconut milk to make a smooth dough. Knead well. Make into small balls and flatten each ball with a fork. After flattening, roll off the fork so that a roll is formed. Deep-fry the rolls in ghee on a gentle heat until golden. Allow to drain and make the syrup. Boil the sugar with the water to make a thick syrup. Put the fried rolls in a dish, sprinkle on the cardamom powder and cover with the syrup.

Bombay Diamonds

2 cups milk
2 cups semolina
2 eggs
flour
ghee for deep-frying
1 cup sugar
1 cup water

Heat the milk and stir in the semolina. Stir together over a gentle heat until the mixture thickens. Allow to cool and stir in the beaten eggs. Flour a pastry board and roller. Take the thick semolina mixture and flour it so that it can be rolled out. Cut into diamond shapes and deep-fry the pastry in hot ghee until golden. Make a thick syrup by boiling the sugar and water. Serve the diamonds with the syrup.

Cakes, Balls and Dumplings

The god, Indra, gave Rama's father three rice balls to be eaten by his three queens. Thereby a son and heir was sure to be born. One of the queens left her rice ball untouched and it was seized by a passing bird. The bird flew with it and dropped it in the jungle where the monkeys lived. It was found by a female monkey who ate it and so conceived. Her baby was Hanuman, the monkey-god, the famous monkey-general of Rama. Hanuman's birthday (Hanuman Jayanti) is celebrated on the full-moon day of Chaitra (March–April).

Rice Balls

225 g (½ lb) rice
1 litre (2 pints) milk
2 tablespoons sugar
small stick cinnamon
grated coconut

Wash the rice and leave to soak for an hour. Drain and pour on the milk. Put in the sugar and cinnamon, and simmer gently until the rice is cooked and the milk is absorbed. Leave the thick rice to cool. Make up into small balls with the help of a little ghee on the hands. Roll in coconut, and serve with cream (malai) and sugar if desired. The balls may also be flavoured with other spices such as cardamom and rolled in the powder or in ground pistachio nuts.

Sweet Potato Balls

225 g (½ lb) sweet potatoes, boiled, peeled and mashed
4 cardamoms, skinned and powdered
1 tablespoon grated jaggery or brown sugar
1 tablespoon grated coconut
½ teaspoon salt
2 tablespoons rice flour
ghee for deep-frying

Mix the potato with cardamom, sugar, coconut and salt. Form into small balls. Make a batter with the rice flour and a little water. Dip the balls in the batter and deep-fry in hot ghee until golden. Serve hot. This recipe is from South India.

Banana Balls

3–4 ripe bananas
ghee
1 tablespoon rice flour
1 tablespoon almonds, blanched and sliced
1 tablespoon cashewnuts, sliced
1 tablespoon sultanas
2 tablespoons brown sugar
pinch of ground cinnamon
2 cardamoms, skinned and powdered
1 dessertspoon poppy seeds

Peel the bananas and gently fry in two tablespoons of ghee. Remove from the pan and mash. Stir in the rice flour. Knead to make a dough, adding more rice flour if necessary. Make into small balls and keep aside. Lightly fry the nuts and sultanas in ghee. Add the sugar, cinnamon, cardamom and poppy seeds. Mix together. Make a depression in each banana ball and stuff with the nut mixture. Roll up again, using more rice flour, and deep-fry in ghee. Serve hot.

Sesame Balls

225 g (½ lb) sesame seeds
1 tablespoon peanuts
225 g (½ lb) jaggery or brown sugar
1 tablespoon ghee
1 tablespoon pistachios, ground
1 tablespoon sultanas, fried
6 cardamoms, skinned and powdered

Roast the sesame seeds and peanuts on a tava or hot pan until the seeds begin to turn golden. Grind the peanuts. Melt the jaggery with the ghee and add all the ingredients. Allow to cool until the mixture can be handled. Make up into small balls with the help of a little ghee on the hands. This recipe is from Andhra Pradesh.

Gram Flour Balls (*Besan laddū*)

On the fourth day of Bhadrapad (August–September), Ganesh Chaturthi, the festival of Ganesh is celebrated. The elephant-headed god of knowledge and success is worshipped with great splendour, especially in the Bombay area. Laddus, sweets made from gram flour, are offered to the image of the god of plenty in memory of the story of his creation. Lord Shiva's wife, Parvati, took an oil bath and rubbed the oil from her body with the aid of some gram flour. She then modelled the figure of a child from the lumps of oil-saturated flour. She placed the child outside the bathroom as an attendant (*gana*) where he was later encountered by Shiva. The child, Ganesh, would not allow Shiva to enter the bathroom who thereupon angrily slashed off the child's head. Shiva searched in vain for the head to console his weeping wife, and he eventually substituted the head of an elephant. The gana came to life again and was given the place of head (*pati*) of the attendants or ganas. For this reason, Ganesh is also known as Ganapati. Ganesh later performed many good deeds and is now worshipped as the god of success, particularly by business men. It is considered both auspicious and very necessary to begin all undertakings of importance with a puja for Ganesh.

4 tablespoons ghee
225 g (8 oz) gram flour
6 cardamoms, skinned and powdered
225 g (8 oz) brown sugar
2 tablespoons pistachios, chopped

Heat the ghee and gradually add the flour. Fry until golden. Remove from heat and add the cardamom, sugar and nuts. Mix well, allow to cool and form into balls, with the help of a little ghee on the hands.

Another besan laddu recipe from Maharashtra uses semolina along with the gram flour:

2 cups semolina
2 cups gram flour (besan)
4 tablespoons ghee
2 cups full-cream milk powder
1 cup brown sugar
2 cups icing sugar
10 cardamoms, skinned and powdered
10 almonds, blanched and sliced
½ tablespoon cashewnuts, sliced
½ tablespoon sultanas, fried and sliced

Fry the semolina in 3 tablespoons of ghee until golden. Do the same with the gram flour. Make up khoya by adding a little water to the powdered milk. Now mix the flours together, add another tablespoon of ghee and fry the mixture until the khoya is browned. Mix in the rest of the ingredients and stir well to make smooth. Allow to cool until the mixture can be formed in the hands into small balls (laddus) with the help of a little ghee. Allow to turn hard before serving.

Green Gram Balls (*Mūng dāl laddū*)

500 g (1 lb) green gram (mung dal)
500 g (1 lb) jaggery or brown sugar
2 cups water
½ cup grated coconut
10 cardamoms, skinned and powdered
1½ tablespoons wholewheat flour (ata)
rice flour

Wash the dal, drain and roast on a tava or hot pan till golden. Grind to a powder. Make a syrup with the sugar and water by boiling to one-thread consistency. Stir in the coconut and cardamom, and continue simmering the syrup very gently. Mix the ground dal with the wholewheat flour and stir into the syrup mixture. When well mixed and thick, start making up the laddus with the hot mixture with the aid of a little rice flour or ghee. Only allow to cool when all the laddus are made. This recipe is from South India.

Yellow Gram Balls (*Dāl laddū*)

500 g (1 lb) yellow gram (channa dal)
4 tablespoons ghee
225 g (8 oz) khoya
1 cup icing sugar
½ cup brown sugar
½ tablespoon almonds, blanched and sliced
½ tablespoon pistachios, chopped
10 cardamoms, skinned and powdered

Wash the dal and leave to soak for a few hours. Drain carefully and grind to a paste. Heat the ghee and fry the dal paste until golden. Put in the khoya (see under Basic Ingredients), and fry until this is browned and the mixture is smooth. Add the rest of the ingredients and stir well to make smooth. Allow to cool until the mixture can be formed in the hands into laddus with the help of a little ghee. Allow to turn hard before serving. This recipe is from Maharashtra.

Black Gram Balls (*Urhad dāl laddū*)

500 g (1 lb) black gram (urhad dal)
ghee for deep-frying
500 g (1 lb) sugar
2 cups water or milk
1 tablespoon almonds, blanched and chopped
1 tablespoon pistachios, chopped
1 tablespoon poppy seeds
10 cardamoms, skinned and powdered

Wash the dal and leave to soak in water for a few hours. Drain and grind to a smooth paste. Heat the ghee and allow drops of the dal paste to pass through a sieve to be fried like bundi. Fry the drops until golden, but do not overcook. Drain and keep aside. Make a thick syrup by boiling the sugar with the water. Care must be taken if sugar and milk are used. When the syrup thickens add the fried paste drops and the rest of the ingredients, and cook gently until the thick mixture leaves the sides of the pan. Allow to cool until the mixture can be formed into laddus with the aid of a little ghee if necessary. Cool before serving. These laddus are from Uttar Pradesh.

Semolina Balls (*Sūji laddū*)

Ganesha is represented with four hands. In one he holds a gourd, in the second a laddu, in the third an axe and in the fourth a rosary. He has a yellow garment and he rides a mouse. His favourite dish is sweet-balls of wheat flour fried in ghee and sweetened with molasses.

- 225 g (8 oz) semolina
- 1 tablespoon ghee
- 225 g (8 oz) molasses, grated jaggery or brown sugar
- 250 ml (½ pint) milk
- 1 tablespoon cashewnuts, chopped
- 1 tablespoon sultanas, fried in ghee
- 10 cardamoms, skinned and powdered

Fry the semolina in a pan on a low heat in the ghee until it turns golden. Add the sugar, milk, nuts and sultanas and cook on a low heat, stirring continuously until a thick lump is formed. Allow to cool. Make up into small balls with the aid of a little ghee on the hands. Arrange the laddus on a dish and sprinkle with the cardamom powder. This recipe is from Maharashtra, a state where Ganesh is particularly honoured.

Coconut Balls (*Nareal laddū*)

- 2½ cups grated coconut
- 225 g (8 oz) brown sugar
- 1 litre (2 pints) milk
- 8 cardamoms, skinned and powdered
- 1 tablespoon almonds, blanched and sliced
- 1 tablespoon pistachios, chopped
- 2 tablespoons sultanas, fried in ghee
- pinch of saffron, dissolved in milk

Put the coconut, sugar and milk in a pan and cook on a gentle heat until the mixture thickens. Add the rest of the ingredients and continue cooking, stirring continuously until a thick lump is formed which leaves the sides of the pan. Allow to cool and form into laddus. Serve cooled. These laddus are from Bengal.

Semolina and Coconut Balls (*Sūji nareal laddū*)

500 g (1 lb) semolina
4 tablespoons ghee
1 cup grated coconut
225 g (8 oz) khoya
500 g (1 lb) sugar
10 cardamoms, skinned and powdered
1 tablespoon almonds, blanched and sliced
1 tablespoon pistachios, chopped
1 tablespoon sultanas, fried in ghee
pinch of saffron, dissolved in milk

Fry the semolina in 3 tablespoons of ghee until golden. Do the same with the coconut. Add another tablespoon of ghee and add the khoya (see *khoya* under Basic Ingredients) which is fried until brown. Mix well until the mixture is smooth and stir in the rest of the ingredients. Allow to cool until the thick mixture can be formed into laddus with the aid of a little ghee if necessary.

Peanut Balls (*Kadlekai laddū*)

500 g (1 lb) peanuts
500 g (1 lb) grated jaggery or brown sugar
2 tablespoons ghee
10 cardamoms, skinned and powdered
1 teaspoon poppy seeds
rice flour

Roast the peanuts gently on a tava or hot pan. Grind to a powder. Make a thick syrup by melting the sugar in the ghee. Mix in the rest of the ingredients to make a thick mixture. Allow to cool. Make up into laddus with the help of a little rice flour or ghee. Serve cold. These laddus are from South India. They may be rolled in grated coconut while still warm before serving.

Bundi Balls (*Bundi laddū*)

These traditional laddus, especially popular in western India, are made by pressing the bundi together to form laddus after soaking them in syrup.

1½ cups gram flour (besan)
½ teaspoon baking powder
1 teaspoon ghee
½ cup milk
½ teaspoon saffron, dissolved in warm water
1½ cups sugar
1½ cups water
8 cardamoms, skinned
ghee for deep-frying

Sift the flour and baking powder together and rub in the ghee. Add the milk and enough water to make a thick batter. Stir in half of the saffron water. Now make a syrup in a separate pan by boiling the sugar with the water until thick. A drop will form a small ball on the edge of a cold plate. Stir in the cardamom seeds and keep the syrup warm. Now the bundis have to be fried quickly. Put a spoonful of batter on a slice or large-holed sieve and tap the batter into the hot ghee. The bundi should quickly fry to golden but should not burn, so now is the time to adjust the heat if necessary. Make batches of bundi, remove from the ghee with a strainer and put in the thick syrup. The rest of the saffron can be added to colour and flavour the syrup. When all of the bundi have been put in and the syrup is used up, portions of the mixture should be made up into balls by pressing together in the hands. A little ghee or rice flour on the hands will make the job easier. Serve cold. These laddus look very nice with a sprinkling of ground pistachio nut on the top. Add this before they are completely cooled.

Rice and Coconut Balls

1 cup rice
salt
1 cup grated coconut
ghee
honey or melted jaggery

Wash the rice and leave to soak for an hour. Boil the rice until quite soft and pliable. Sprinkle with a pinch of salt and mix well with the coconut. Allow to cool, form portions of the mixture into small balls. Arrange on a dish and pour over melted ghee and honey to serve. Ground pistachio may be added as a garnish. This simple sweet is made in Mangalore, South India.

Bundi Balls with Nuts (*Darvesh*)

2 tablespoons rice flour
2 tablespoons semolina
pinch baking powder
½ teaspoon saffron, dissolved in water
1 cup sugar
1 cup water
ghee for deep-frying
1 cup khoya
1 tablespoon almonds, blanched and sliced
1 tablespoon sultanas, fried in ghee
8 cardamoms, skinned and powdered
1 tablespoon pistachios, ground

Make up a batter by mixing the rice flour, semolina and baking powder with enough water. Mix in half of the saffron water. Leave to stand. Now make a syrup by boiling the sugar and water for a few minutes. Add the rest of the saffron water. Make bundi with the batter as in the recipe for bundi balls. Put the bundi in the syrup and mix in the rest of the ingredients except the pistachios. Form the mixture into small balls when cool enough and sprinkle each with some pistachio. These laddus are made in Bengal.

Sweet Flour Balls (*Sato*)

1 cup wholewheat flour
1 tablespoon rice flour
1 tablespoon gram flour (besan)
2 tablespoons ghee
2 cups sugar
1 cup water
4 cardamoms, skinned

Sift the flours together and rub in the ghee. Add enough water to make a stiff dough. Make up the dough into walnut-sized balls and deep-fry in ghee until golden. Make a thick syrup by boiling the sugar with the water and cardamom seeds. Put in the balls, coat well with syrup, remove and allow the sugar to frost.

Milk Cakes (*Dūdh perha*)

1 cup khoya
1 cup sugar
2 tablespoons pistachios, ground
8 cardamoms, skinned and powdered

Mix the khoya (see *khoya* under Basic Ingredients) with the sugar in a pan and heat gently to blend. When a smooth, pliable mixture is formed, shape portions to form small balls. Flatten each ball in the hand to make a biscuit which must not be too thin. Arrange the perhas on a greased dish and sprinkle on the pistachio and cardamom.

Sugared Doughnuts (*Bālūshāhi*)

2 teaspoons baking powder
2 cups wholewheat flour
ghee
1 cup sugar
1 cup water
few drops red colouring

Sift together the baking powder and flour. Work in 3 tablespoons of ghee and add enough water to make a soft dough. Make up into small balls, flatten each one to make a doughnut shape and make a hole in the centre. Make a thick syrup by boiling the sugar and water. Stir in the red colouring. Now gently deep-fry the balushahis in ghee. Heat the ghee, then remove from the heat. Slip in a balushahi and allow to cook until the ghee stops simmering. Put the pan back on the heat and repeat the process until the balushahi is well risen and golden. Shake the pan occasionally. Place each balushahi in a sieve and slowly pour over the hot thick syrup so that it soaks well in. Allow to cool. When served they should be well coated with sugar. For an extra treat serve with chopped nuts and cream with a little rosewater in the syrup.

Thick Milk Cakes (*Pinni*)

1 cup wholewheat flour (ata)
2 tablespoons ghee
½ cup caster sugar or brown sugar
1 heaped tablespoon khoya
1 tablespoon almonds, blanched and sliced
1 tablespoon sultanas, fried in ghee
8 cardamoms, skinned and powdered

Fry the flour gently in the ghee until the ghee begins to separate out from the flour. Do not allow the flour to brown too much. Stir in the rest of the ingredients (see *khoya* under Basic Ingredients). The mixture should be stiff enough to form into small balls like laddus. Flatten the balls and arrange on a dish before serving. Pinnis can be made with other flours such as besan and urhad dal flour. The khoya may be substituted with grated coconut. This recipe is from Northern India.

Rice Cakes (*Koikotai*)

500 g (1 lb) rice flour
½ cup sugar
coconut milk
1 tablespoon pistachios, ground

Mix the flour with the sugar, and add enough coconut milk or creamed coconut to make a stiff dough. Form the mixture into small balls and steam. Koikotai are made by the Tamil people at christening or naming time. They can be stuffed with grated coconut, jaggery or brown sugar and a little powdered cardamom seed.

Sweet Dumplings (*Mīthe idli*)

1 cup black gram (urhad dal)
1 cup rice
½ cup grated jaggery or brown sugar
8 cardamoms, skinned and powdered

Wash the gram and rice and leave to soak for a few hours or overnight. Drain and grind each to a paste. Mix the sugar with a cup of water and heat gently till the sugar dissolves. Stir in the cardamom and gram and rice pastes. Mix well and leave to stand for an hour. Take some small katoris (metal bowls) or small china bowls, grease well with some ghee or butter and fill three-quarters full with the idli batter. Steam until the idlis are firm. When a fork is inserted it should come out clean. Serve with warm milk, coconut milk or cream. These dumplings are very nice with stewed fruit.

Idlis, a favourite dish in South India, may be very nicely stuffed. Mix a cup of grated coconut with half a cup of sugar, a tablespoon of finely chopped nuts and some fried sultanas, sliced. This time fill the little bowls half full with the idli batter. Spread on some of the filling mixture and fill up with some more batter. Steam in the usual way. Another method is to mix some nice ingredients with the batter itself. Idlis provide a good dish for experimentation.

Stuffed Patties (*Modak*)

2 cups rice
1 teaspoon ghee
½ teaspoon salt
½ coconut or equivalent grated coconut
10 almonds, blanched and sliced
1 tablespoon raisins or sultanas
4 cardamoms, crushed
1½ tablespoons sugar

Wash the rice and soak for fifteen minutes. Drain and grind to a powder. Mix in the ghee and salt. Measure the powdered rice and boil in an equal amount of water over a low heat, stirring constantly to prevent lumps forming. Cook until a soft doughy consistency is obtained. Mix the coconut, almonds, raisins and cardamoms with the sugar, and cook on a low heat until the sugar melts and this stuffing mixture is fairly dry. Roll out the dough and make saucer-sized rounds. Put some stuffing mixture on to the rounds and roll up to form a cone. Seal and steam until the pastry is cooked.

Modakam is offered to Lord Ganesha in Tamilnadu temples.

Biscuits

Rice and Coconut Biscuits

3 cups rice flour
½ cup brown sugar
2 cups grated coconut
6 cardamoms, skinned and powdered

Sift together the flour, sugar, coconut and cardamom powder. Make into a stiff dough by adding boiling water a little at a time. Knead well. Make the dough into small balls and flatten to make biscuits. Bake on both sides on a greased tava or hot pan.

Rice Flour Biscuits

2 cups rice flour
1 tablespoon poppy seeds
10 cardamoms, skinned and powdered
pinch of salt
2 cups grated jaggery or brown sugar
2 cups water
ghee for frying

Mix the flour, poppy seeds, cardamom and salt in a pan. Make a syrup by boiling the sugar and water for a few minutes. Now pour the syrup on to the flour mixture. Stir well until a thick doughy mixture is formed. Cover and keep overnight. Next day knead again and form the dough into small balls. Flatten each ball to make biscuits and fry in ghee on both sides until golden. Drain and serve with cream.

Nankhatai

3 tablespoons ghee
½ cup brown sugar
1 teaspoon yogurt
1 cup wholewheat flour (ata)
¼ teaspoon baking powder
10 cardamoms, skinned and powdered
pistachios or blanched almonds, halved

Cream the ghee with the sugar and beat in the yogurt. Sift together the flour, baking powder and cardamom. Add the creamed sugar. Knead the mixture well and squeeze into 12–15 balls. Flatten each one slightly and press on a half nut. Put the nankhatais on a greased baking tray and leave to stand for 1–2 hours. Bake for 20–25 minutes at 335°F or medium oven until lightly browned. Nankhatais are a hard biscuit. Allow to cool and store in an airtight tin. This recipe is from Northern India.

Anarasa

3 cups rice flour
1 cup grated jaggery or brown sugar
2 tablespoons icing sugar
ghee
½ tablespoon almonds, blanched and ground
½ tablespoon pistachios, ground
1 tablespoon poppy seeds
10 cardamoms, skinned and powdered
1 teaspoon rosewater

Mix the flour with the sugar and add enough melted ghee to form a smooth stiff dough. Make up the dough into small balls. Cover and keep aside for 2–3 days. Knead the balls again. Pound the nuts, poppy seeds and cardamom together, and add enough rosewater to help bind the mixture. Flatten the dough balls to make biscuits and press some of the nut mixture on to each biscuit. Carefully fry in ghee until golden. Drain and allow to cool. Store in an airtight container. These biscuits are from Western India.

Khaja

500 g (1 lb) wholewheat flour
10 cardamoms, skinned and powdered
¼ teaspoon baking powder
pinch of saffron, dissolved in water
1 cup sugar
1 cup water
ghee for frying

Sift together the flour, cardamom and baking powder. Mix in the saffron with a little water. Make a syrup by boiling the sugar with water for a few minutes. Add the syrup to the flour mixture and knead to make a smooth, stiff dough. Leave to stand for an hour. Make the dough into small balls, flatten to form biscuits and fry in ghee on both sides until golden. Store when cool in an airtight container. These biscuits come from Maharashtra.

Gaja

2 cups wholewheat flour (ata)
4 tablespoons ghee
4 tablespoons icing sugar
2 teaspoons poppy seeds
ghee for deep-frying

Sift the flour and rub in the ghee. Add the sugar and poppy seeds and enough water to make a smooth pastry dough. Knead well and roll out to make finger-size biscuits. Deep-fry in ghee until golden. Allow to cool and store in an airtight container. These biscuits are from Bengal.

Kerala Kalkals

500 g (1 lb) rice flour
3 tablespoons urhad dal flour
coconut milk or creamed coconut
½ cup sugar
½ cup water
4 cardamoms, crushed
ghee for deep-frying

Sift together the flours and add enough coconut milk to make a soft, smooth dough. Make a thick syrup by boiling the sugar and water together with the cardamom pods. Make the dough into very small balls. Take a ball and flatten it out on a fork. Now roll the piece of dough off so that the fork pattern is nicely imprinted and a little roll shape is formed. Deep-fry the kalkals in ghee until golden, taking care not to overcook. Drain and put in the thick syrup to frost. Remove from the syrup and allow the kalkals to dry. Store in an airtight container.

The Snake-Charmer's Tale

The beggars all applauded the tale of the gardener and shouted for more. Hearing about the mongoose had reminded one of the others about the day he lost his snakes, for the mongoose is noted for his courage in attacking the cobra.

'It was God's will that I should be blinded by disease,' he began. 'For this reason I have tried to see all the more clearly with my other senses, though events in my life have made this difficult, I can tell you.'

This sentiment met with approving noises from the others. The story of a fellow-sufferer was always worth the hearing.

'My mother was desperate,' he continued, 'since my father had just died when I became blind and we wondered what I would do for work. As luck would have it, a snake-charmer called at our village the following week. After his performance he astonished all of us present by announcing that it would be his last. "I am renouncing all to become a sadhu," he shouted in his high voice. Some were disappointed, but the general feeling was of admiration for the man since the sadhu's life is not an easy one.

'Anyway, you can imagine my shock when he turned in my direction and spoke to me. "That blind man over there will be my successor," said he. "I will teach him all I know so that he may carry on my work for me." There was a great cheer, then I felt my mother tugging at my arm. "Come away," she whispered, "no good can come of those snakes!" Naturally, I felt this was my lucky day. For some reason I was having the prospect of a permanent job put in my very hands. A blind man cannot afford to say no to such luck.' The beggars growled their approval.

'So there I was, my friends. After some weeks I could play the flute and charm the snakes. But I'll let you into a secret – they are quite deaf, they can't hear any more than we can see! At first I did well in the trade. I took to the road with my mother and between us we made a modest living. Then one day we arrived at this village. As soon as we had sat down the village headman appeared. His voice did not sound at all welcoming. "Go away from here," he shouted. "No good will come from your visit. We have a sick person here who has a dire fear of the serpent. He will surely do you harm!"

'My mother urged me to get up and proceed on our way, but I was tired and hungry from the long walk and I could feel the cool of the evening descending. "May we just rest the night here, then?" I asked. The headman agreed. "But see you leave before sunrise. I have a hut near here where you can sleep."

'That night I had a strange dream. The serpents came out of their baskets and spoke to me. "Set us free and we will be your eyes," they said. I answered them, saying, "If I let you be my eyes, I will surely lose my hearing for I know that you are deaf. I dare not take the risk." "So be it," said the serpents, and they returned to their baskets. My sleep must have been fitful and I awoke before dawn. After rousing my mother, I went to check the snake baskets only to find that they had been tampered with. The serpents were gone!'

At this point in the story, the beggars leaned forward eager to hear what was to follow. 'What had happened?' breathed one.

'I met the headman outside. He was not at all sympathetic. "My snakes are gone. I shall be worse than a beggar without them," I told him. Just then one of the villagers arrived sounding very flustered. "It's Avidya. He stole the snakes and killed them! He says he cannot allow them to hear his conversation or they will curse him." "I warned you," shouted the headman. "Avidya cannot stand the thought of the snakes listening to what he says." "But they cannot hear what he says," I protested. "The serpent folk are deaf!"

'It was shortly after that that my mother and I were reduced to beggary.'

Pastries

Davachi Chauth is the fourth day of the first fortnight of the month of Shravan (July–August), sacred to Ganesh and his mother. Yellow and red silk amulets are prepared to correspond with the number of boys and girls in the family. Sweets and pastries are made and a celebration takes place. Red silk amulets are tied to the arms of the boys to represent Ganesh, and yellow amulets are tied to the girls to represent his mother. Later the pastries and sweets are distributed amongst the family and friends.

Sweet Samosa

1½ cups wholewheat flour
ghee
4 tablespoons ground almonds or khoya
2 tablespoons sultanas, fried in ghee
2 tablespoons brown sugar
10 cardamoms, skinned and powdered

Sieve the flour and rub in 2 tablespoons of melted ghee. Add enough water (about 5 tablespoons) to make a smooth dough. Knead for ten minutes, cover with a damp cloth and allow to stand. Now mix the stuffing ingredients together with a little milk or cream to bind. Knead together. Knead the dough again and make into small balls. Roll out each ball quite thinly and cut in half. Lay the pieces over each other, press together and roll out as thin as possible to form a semicircle. Put a portion of the filling mixture in one half of the semicircle, moisten the edges and fold the other half over. Press the edges well together, and deep-fry in hot ghee until crisp and golden. Serve hot or cold with cream or yogurt.

Sweet Dal Samosa

1½ cups wholewheat flour
ghee
1 cup red lentils (masur dal)
4 cardamoms, crushed
2 cloves
small piece cinnamon
2 tablespoons brown sugar
2 tablespoons grated coconut

Make up the samosa dough as in the previous recipe and make into small balls. Cover while the filling mixture is prepared. Wash the dal and boil with just enough water to cook until soft. Put the cardamom, cloves and cinnamon in with the water. When the lentils are soft, drain off any excess liquid and remove the spices. Stir in the sugar and coconut. If the filling is still too damp, heat gently in a pan to remove the moisture. Put the filling in the samosas as in the previous recipe. Deep-fry as before.

Coconut Samosa

- 1½ cups wholewheat flour
- ghee
- 1 cup grated coconut
- 4 cardamoms, skinned and powdered
- 2 tablespoons brown sugar
- 2 tablespoons sultanas, fried in ghee
- 1 tablespoon pistachios, finely chopped

Make up the samosa dough as before and make into small balls. Cover while the filling mixture is prepared. Mix the ingredients together and lightly fry in ghee for a few minutes. Put the filling in the samosas as in the previous recipes. Deep-fry as before. Drain and serve hot or cold.

Banana Samosa

- 1½ cups wholewheat flour
- ghee
- 1 cup mashed, ripe bananas
- 1 cup grated coconut
- 2 tablespoons brown sugar
- pinch of saffron, dissolved in a little milk

Make up the samosa dough as in the previous recipes, and make into small balls. Cover while the filling mixture is prepared. Mix the bananas, coconut, sugar and saffron. Fry in a little ghee until a thick mixture is formed. Put the filling as in the previous recipes. Deep-fry the samosas, drain and serve hot or cold with cream or yogurt.

Puffed Pastry with Gram Stuffing (*Puran poli*)

In Western India the spring equinox and the wheat harvest occur at the same time. Bonfires are built and it is a time of great jollity and boisterous behaviour. This is the time of the Holi festival. One of the customs is to throw coloured powder over whoever you meet in the street, or to squirt people with bicycle pumps filled with coloured water. Consequently only the oldest clothes are worn. The bonfires are called *holis*, and celebrations may go on all night. Puran poli is a symbolic pastry made at this time. Since the holis are worshipped as goddesses, puran poli may be thrown into the fire with a coconut as a sacrifice to them.

2 cups wholewheat flour
ghee
1½ cups lentils (masur dal)
½ cup grated jaggery or brown sugar
1 cup grated coconut
1 tablespoon poppy seed
1 tablespoon sesame seed
4 cardamoms, skinned and powdered

Sift the dough and rub in two tablespoons of ghee. Add enough water to make a smooth dough. Make into small balls and leave to stand. Now make up the stuffing. Wash the lentils and boil with a little water until soft and almost dry. Drain off the excess liquid and add the sugar, stir well. Fry the coconut, poppy seeds, sesame seeds and cardamom in a little ghee until the coconut begins to turn golden. Mix in with the lentils and sugar. If the filling mixture is still a little damp, heat gently to drive off the excess moisture. Roll out the dough balls and put a portion of the filling mixture in the centre of one. Cover with another and roll out to make a thick puri. Fry each one in ghee until golden, drain and serve hot or cold with cream or yogurt. These puris are sometimes known as poli puri.

Puffed Pastry with Thick Milk (*Khoya poli*)

225 g (½ lb) wholewheat flour
1½ tablespoons ghee
milk
2 tablespoons khoya
2 tablespoons grated coconut
1 tablespoon sugar
1 tablespoon sultanas, fried in ghee
1 tablespoon almonds, blanched and finely chopped
4 cardamoms, skinned and powdered
2 teaspoons rosewater

Sift the flour and rub in the ghee. Add enough milk or water to make a smooth dough. Make into small balls and leave to stand. Now make up the stuffing. Mix all the ingredients together and work the rosewater well in. Place some filling on the rolled out dough and make up the polis as in the previous recipe. Fry in ghee until golden, drain and serve hot or cold with cream or yogurt. These polis or puris are from Gujerat.

Puffed Pastry with Coconut (*Nareal poli*)

225 g (½ lb) wholewheat flour
1½ tablespoons ghee
2 cups grated coconut
1 cup brown sugar
6 cardamoms, skinned and powdered
1 tablespoon rosewater

Sift the flour and rub in the ghee. Add enough water to make a smooth dough. Make into small balls and leave to stand. Mix the filling ingredients together in a pan over a gentle heat until the sugar melts and binds the ingredients. Roll out the dough balls and make up polis as in the recipe for Puran poli.

Puffed Pastry with Cashewnuts (*Kaju poli*)

225 g (½ lb) wholewheat flour
pinch of salt
1½ tablespoons ghee
1 cup cashewnuts
4 cardamoms, skinned and powdered
2 teaspoons rosewater
½ cup sugar

Sift the flour and salt together and rub in the ghee. Add enough water to form a smooth dough. Make into small balls and leave to stand. Pound the cashewnuts with the cardamom and rosewater. Mix with the sugar in a pan over a gentle heat so that the sugar melts and binds the filling. Roll out the dough balls and make up polis as in the recipe for puran poli. Fry in ghee until golden, drain and serve hot or cold with cream or yogurt. These two polis are from Maharashtra.

Banana Puffs

225 g (½ lb) wholewheat flour
pinch salt
1½ tablespoons ghee
2–3 ripe bananas, peeled and mashed
½ cup grated coconut
3 cardamoms, skinned and powdered

Sift the flour and salt and rub in the ghee. Add enough water or milk to make a smooth dough. Make into small balls and leave to stand. Mix the bananas, coconut and cardamom well. Roll out the balls and put a portion of the banana mixture on one half of a round. Moisten the edges and fold over to make a half-moon shape. Seal the edges. Deep-fry in ghee until golden. Drain and serve hot or cold. A pinch of baking powder may be added to the dough to make it puff up still more. The banana mixture may be fried in a little ghee before being used as a filling. Drain off the excess ghee.

Holige with Gram Stuffing (*Dāl holige*)

225 g (½ lb) semolina
4 tablespoons plain flour
pinch baking powder
pinch salt
3–4 tablespoons ghee or sesame oil
¾ cup lentils (masur dal)
1 cup grated coconut
1 cup grated jaggery or brown sugar
10 cardamoms, skinned and powdered

Sift together the semolina, flour, baking powder and salt. Rub in the ghee and add enough water to make a smooth dough. Make up into small balls and leave to stand. Wash the dal and boil with a little water until soft and dry. Mix in the coconut and sugar. Heat gently in a pan until all the ingredients are well blended and stir in the cardamom. Roll out the dough balls as thinly as possible with the help of a little plain flour or ghee. Place a portion of the filling mixture on one half of the round, fold over and seal up the edges. Fry in ghee until golden. Drain and serve hot with milk, cream or yogurt.

Poppy Seed Holige (*Mandige holige*)

225 g (½ lb) semolina
4 tablespoons plain flour
pinch baking powder
pinch salt
3–4 tablespoons ghee or sesame oil
¾ cup poppy seeds
4 tablespoons brown sugar
6 cardamoms, skinned and powdered

Sift together the semolina, flour, baking powder and salt. Rub in the ghee and add enough water to make a smooth dough. Make up into small balls and leave to stand. Grind the poppy seeds, sugar and cardamom. Put in a pan over a gentle heat and add a little ghee to bind the mixture (1–2 teaspoons). Make up the holiges as in the previous recipe and serve in the same way.

Sweet Potato Holige

225 g (½ lb) semolina
4 tablespoons plain flour
pinch baking powder
pinch salt
3–4 tablespoons ghee or sesame oil
1 cup boiled sweet potatoes, peeled and mashed
4 tablespoons brown sugar
1 tablespoon cashewnuts, finely chopped
6 cardamoms, skinned and powdered

Sift together the semolina, flour, baking powder and salt. Rub in the ghee or oil and add enough water to make a smooth dough. Make up into small balls and leave to stand. Mash the sweet potato again with the sugar and mix in the nuts and cardamom. Roll out the dough balls and make up the holiges as in the recipe for Dāl holige. Serve hot in the usual way.

Holiges are from South India. Wholewheat flour may be used instead of plain flour. Traditionally they are made with sesame oil but ghee or other oils may be used. Try experimenting with different fillings to find the one you like best.

Coconut Patties

225 g (½ lb) wholewheat flour
225 g (½ lb) semolina
2 tablespoons ghee
2 egg yolks
½ cup coconut milk or creamed coconut
1 cup grated coconut
½ cup sultanas, fried in ghee
½ cup almonds, blanched and sliced
6 cardamoms, skinned and powdered
4 tablespoons brown sugar

Sift together the flour and semolina. Rub in the ghee then mix in the egg yolks and coconut milk. Knead well to make a dough. Leave to stand. Mix the filling ingredients well over a gentle heat so that the sugar melts and binds the ingredients, Make up the dough into small balls and roll out. Alternatively, roll out the dough and cut out round shapes. Put a portion of the filling on one half of a round, fold over and seal up the edges. Fry in ghee until golden. Serve hot or cold.

Date and Coconut Patties

1½ cups wholewheat flour (ata)
pinch baking powder
ghee
1 cup grated coconut
3 tablespoons poppy seeds
½ cup stoned dates
small piece cinnamon, ground
4 cardamoms, skinned and powdered
4 tablespoons brown sugar

Sift the flour with the baking powder and rub in 2 tablespoons of ghee. Add enough water to make a smooth dough and leave to stand. Fry the coconut and poppy seed in a little ghee and pound with the rest of the filling ingredients. Roll out the dough and cut out squares of pastry. Put a portion of the filling in one half of each square, fold over and seal up the edges. Fry the patties in ghee until golden. Serve hot or cold. These patties are from Western India.

Karanjia

2 cups wholewheat flour
pinch of salt
2 tablespoons ghee
½ cup khoya
1 tablespoon cashewnuts, finely chopped
1 tablespoon sultanas, fried in ghee
½ cup brown sugar
6 cardamoms, skinned and powdered

Karanjias are another form of patty from Western India. Make up the dough by sifting the flour and salt together. Rub in the ghee and add enough water to make a smooth dough. Leave to stand. Mix the filling ingredients well. Roll out the dough and cut out the rounds. Fill in the usual way and make up the patty as in the recipe for Coconut Patties. (See *khoya* under Basic Ingredients.)

Semolina Karanjia (*Sūji karanjia*)

2 cups wholewheat flour (ata)
pinch of salt
2 tablespoons ghee
1 tablespoon cashewnuts, finely chopped
1 tablespoon almonds, blanched and finely chopped
1 tablespoon sultanas
½ cup semolina (suji)
2 tablespoons ghee
½ cup brown sugar
6 cardamoms, skinned and powdered

Make up the dough as in the previous recipe. Gently fry the nuts and sultanas in a little ghee until golden. Now fry the semolina in two tablespoons of ghee until it is golden but not beginning to turn too brown. Mix with the fried nuts and stir in the rest of the filling ingredients over a gentle heat. As soon as the mixture begins to bind allow to cool and fill the karanjias as before. Deep-fry until golden.

Marrow Karanjia (*Gūda karanjia*)

2 cups wholewheat flour (ata)
pinch of salt
2 tablespoons ghee
1 tablespoon cashewnuts, finely chopped
1 tablespoon almonds, blanched and finely chopped
1 tablespoon sultanas
1 tablespoon poppy seeds
2 cups marrow, peeled and cubed
½ cup brown sugar
6 cardamoms, skinned and powdered

Make up the dough as in the recipe for Karanjia. Gently fry the nuts, sultanas and poppy seeds in a little ghee until the nuts are golden. Cook the marrow in minimum water or milk until it is soft. Mash and mix with the sugar and cardamom. Mix in the fried nuts. Heat the filling mixture gently if any moisture needs to be driven off. Fill the karanjias as before and deep-fry in ghee until golden. Any other vegetable like marrow may be used in this recipe. Simply cook the vegetable until it is soft and mix in the rest of the ingredients. The pastry may be changed by using semolina or rice flour or combinations of these flours.

Pastry in Milk (*Chukoli*)

2 cups wholewheat flour
pinch of baking powder
pinch of salt
2 tablespoons ghee

1 litre (2 pints) milk
pinch of saffron
½ cup thick cream
1 tablespoon pistachios, ground

Sift together the flour, baking powder and salt. Rub in the ghee and add enough water or milk to make a smooth dough. Roll out the dough to make thin pastry and cut out small diamond or other shapes. These may be baked a little in a moderate oven or gently fried in ghee. Meanwhile heat the milk with the saffron until it is yellow. Drop in the cooked pastry and boil the milk well. Remove from the heat and spread over the cream. Sprinkle on the pistachios and serve. The pastry may also be cooked in the boiling milk, but it will have to be kept in longer and may be too soft for some tastes.

Sweet Breads

Sita, the wife of the god-king Rama, was born out of the earth by the touch of a plough. The plough is considered sacred because it is the chief implement in cultivation. It is worshipped on the full-moon day of Shravan (July–August). Because of the sanctity of the plough it is auspicious for the plough to be present at wedding ceremonies.

Sweet Bread (*Mīthe roti*)

A simple sweet bread may be made by making a dough from whole-wheat flour, ghee and water and filling with brown sugar or sugared coconut. Roll out a ball of dough. Put some of the sweetening in the centre. Put on another round of rolled dough and carefully roll out a new round, making sure that the filling does not break through.

Bake on a hot plate, tava or pan, like a chapati. This bread will be nice with butter or cream. Here is a recipe with a few more ingredients:

2 cups wholewheat flour
teaspoon of salt
1 cup lentils or other dal
1 cup sugar
6 cardamoms, skinned and powdered

Sift together the flour and salt, and gradually add water until a soft dough is formed. Knead well until the dough is velvety and pliable. Leave to stand. Wash the dal and boil with a little water until it is soft. Drain off any excess moisture and add the sugar and cardamom powder. Stir together and heat the mixture gently until it is dry. Knead the dough and roll out flat. Cut out rounds with a teacup and put a portion of the filling on a round. Cover with another round and roll out carefully, making sure that the filling does not break through. Bake on a hot plate, tava or heavy pan, until golden on both sides.

Rogni Roti

1 cup sugar
½ teaspoon saffron, dissolved in ½ cup warm water
1½ cups wholewheat flour
1 cup semolina
3 tablespoons ghee

Make a syrup by mixing the sugar with the saffron water. Sift together the flour and semolina and rub in the ghee. Make a dough by adding the syrup gradually. Knead well and roll out to pastry thickness. Cut out large round shapes and bake on both sides on a hot plate, tava or heavy pan, until golden.

Royal Bread (*Shāhi tukara*)

6 slices of bread
3–4 tablespoons ghee
½ cup sugar
1 cup cream
1 tablespoon rosewater
10 almonds, blanched and sliced
4 cardamoms, skinned and powdered
1 tablespoon pistachios, ground

Cut the bread into cubes and fry in ghee until golden. Arrange the fried cubes in a dish. Make a syrup by boiling the sugar with 4 tablespoons of water. Pour over the fried cubes and allow to soak. Pour on the cream and rosewater. Sprinkle with the nuts and cardamom. Serve chilled.

Sweet Chapati

Make up a chapati dough as in the recipe for Sweet Bread. Mix up a cupful of brown sugar with a teaspoon of powdered cardamom seeds. Knead this into the dough and roll out thinly. Cut out rounds. Smear a hot plate with ghee, heat well and put on a chapati. When little bubbles begin to appear, put some melted ghee around the edges and turn over to bake on the other side until the bread is nicely puffed up and golden.

Sesame Chapati

2 cups wholewheat flour
2 tablespoons ghee or sesame oil
1 tablespoon gram flour (besan)
2 tablespoons sesame seeds
1 cup grated jaggery or brown sugar

Rub the ghee into the flour and add enough water to make a soft, stiff dough. Leave to stand. Gently roast the gram flour on a hot plate until it begins to turn colour. Now roast the sesame seeds to lightly brown them. Mix the flour and seeds with the sugar and blend well. Knead the dough again and form into small balls. Roll out to form rounds. Put a portion of the sesame mixture on a round and cover with another. Seal up and roll out again carefully to make a chapati as thin as possible, with the aid of a little flour. Bake on a hot plate as in the recipe for Sweet Chapati. Serve spread with butter. Rice flour may be used to make the dough.

Sweet Puri (*Mīthe pūri*)

1½ cups wholewheat flour
ghee
1 cup milk
2 tablespoons sugar
4 cardamoms, skinned and powdered

Rub the flour and 1–2 tablespoons ghee together. Dissolve the sugar in the milk and stir in the cardamom powder. Add the sugared milk to the flour gradually and knead to form a soft, stiff dough. Divide into small balls and roll out with a rolling pin rubbed with ghee. Deep-fry in ghee until the puri is golden and puffed up. Drain and serve hot.

Banana Puri

225 g (½ lb) wholewheat flour
110 g (4 oz) gram flour (besan)
½ teaspoon salt
½ teaspoon powdered cumin seed
ghee
3 ripe bananas, peeled
1 tablespoon brown sugar

Sift together the flours, salt and cumin powder. Rub in 2 tablespoons of melted ghee and knead well. Mash the bananas and mix with the sugar. Add this to the flour and knead well. Divide into small balls and make puris as in the previous recipe. These puris may also be baked like a chapati on a hot plate. Serve hot.

Sesame Puri

1½ cups wholewheat flour
½ teaspoon salt
1 tablespoon sesame seeds
1 tablespoon soft brown sugar
1 teaspoon caraway seeds
ghee

Sift together the flour and salt. Lightly roast the sesame seeds and grind to a powder. Mix in the sugar and caraway seeds and add this to the flour. Rub in two tablespoons ghee and add enough water to make a soft, stiff dough. Roll out and cut out small puris, or form into small balls and roll out. Deep-fry the puris in ghee until golden and puffed up. Serve hot.

Yellow Gram Paratha (*Channa dāl parātha*)

1½ cups yellow gram (channa dal)
2 cups wholewheat flour (ata)
1 tablespoon sesame oil or ghee
1 cup brown sugar
8 cardamoms, skinned and powdered
2 cloves, ground
ghee

Wash the dal and leave to soak overnight in water. Next day, rub the oil into the flour and add enough water to make a soft, stiff dough.

Knead well. Boil the dal in a little water until soft. Mash well and stir in the sugar and ground spices. Heat the mixture gently to drive off any excess moisture. Roll out the dough to make balls and put a portion of the filling into the centre. Roll into a ball again and roll out to make a thick pancake. Bake on a hot plate, tava or heavy pan, well smeared with ghee. Add more ghee and turn the paratha over and bake the other side. Serve hot spread with butter.

Jaggery Dosa

1 cup grated jaggery or brown sugar
1 cup wholewheat flour
½ cup rice flour
½ cup grated coconut
8 cardamoms, skinned and powdered

Soak the sugar in a cup of warm water and allow to dissolve. Sift together the flours, coconut and cardamom and stir in the syrup to form a thick batter. It is important that the batter be of the right consistency. Add a little water or milk or extra flour accordingly. The dosa is now cooked like a thin pancake. Heat a pancake pan or tava and spread it with a little ghee. Put on a spoonful of the batter and allow to cook like a pancake. Carefully turn and cook on both sides. If any of the dosa gets stuck to the plate, remove before cooking the next one. This dosa is from South India and may be eaten in the morning for breakfast with honey or treacle and a little milk or cream.

Banana Fritter

2 ripe bananas
½ teaspoon baking powder
3 tablespoons wholewheat flour
2 tablespoons brown sugar
1 teaspoon powdered cardamom seed
milk
ghee or oil for frying
lemon

Mash the bananas and mix with the baking powder, flour, sugar and cardamom. Add enough milk to form a thick batter and beat well. Heat a little ghee in a pan and fry spoonfuls of the batter until golden on both sides. Serve hot with lemon juice and more sugar or honey if required.

South Indian Banana Fritter (*Neyyappam*)

These fritters are said to be the favoured food of Lord Ganesha and almost all the gods.

- 675 g (1½ lb) jaggery or brown sugar
- 4 cups rice flour
- ½ coconut or equivalent grated coconut
- 2 bananas, peeled and mashed
- ghee

Melt the sugar in enough water to make a thin syrup. Add the rice flour and grate in the coconut. Add the mashed bananas and two tablespoons of ghee and mix thoroughly. Stir the batter well and fry spoonfuls in ghee to make golden fritters.

In South India the batter would be put in an appam mould. The depressions in the mould are first half-filled with melted ghee. The mould is then heated and the depressions filled with the sweet batter. When the appams are browned on both sides they are removed from the mould.

Sweet Potato Fritter

- ½ kilo (just over a pound) sweet potatoes
- 1 teaspoon butter
- 3 eggs
- 110 g (4 oz) plain flour
- 1 tablespoon brown sugar
- pinch of salt
- milk
- ghee or oil for frying

Boil the sweet potatoes, peel and mash them. Stir in the butter and break the eggs over this. Mix in the flour, sugar and salt. Mix together well and now add enough milk to make a smooth batter. Fry spoonfuls of the batter on a tava or heavy pan on both sides like fritters. Sprinkle with sugar and serve hot. For a slightly different taste use coconut milk or creamed coconut instead of milk.

Puddings

After the god-king Rama had slain the demon Ravana, he started back from Sri Lanka on the triumphant return to his capital on the day now known as Dasara. In former times the elephants and horses of the maharajas would be washed and groomed to take part in a special puja and later on a grand parade. On Dasara day, workers worship the tools of their trade as heavenly gifts. These will include such things as the corn sieve, the winnowing basket, the rice pounder, the plough and the sickle. All such articles are considered sacred so that their touch gives sanctity. The sieve is always worshipped before sweets are prepared for a wedding.

Creamed Rice (*Khīr*)

1 cup rice
1 tablespoon ghee or butter
1 litre (2 pints) milk
4 tablespoons sugar
pinch of saffron, dissolved in warm milk
1 tablespoon rosewater
1 tablespoon almonds, blanched and sliced
1 tablespoon sultanas, fried in ghee
6 cardamoms, skinned and powdered
1 tablespoon pistachios, ground

Wash the rice and soak in water for half an hour. Drain and fry in ghee for a few minutes until the grains become opaque. Add the milk and bring to the boil, stirring continuously. Lower the heat and simmer until the rice is tender. Add the sugar and saffron dissolved in a little warm milk. Continue simmering until the rice becomes creamy, stirring all the time. Stir in the rosewater, nuts and sultanas. Serve hot, sprinkled with cardamom powder and pistachios. The khir may also be served cold. This dish is often given to the priests on religious occasions. It is a very nourishing dish for children and invalids or those recovering from illness and can be made less rich accordingly.

Creamed Almonds (*Khīr badām*)

2250 ml (4 pints) milk
225 g (½ lb) sugar
350 g (12 oz) ground almonds
pinch of saffron dissolved in a little milk
½ teaspoon powdered cardamom seeds

Heat the milk in a large pan with the sugar, and cook gently until it thickens and begins to form khoya. Stir in the almonds, saffron and cardamom powder. Mix well. Serve hot with fresh hot puris (see Sweet Breads).

Mangalore Khir

1 cup rice
½ cup grated coconut
ghee
½ cup grated jaggery or brown sugar
1½ cups coconut milk or creamed coconut
1 teaspoon powdered cardamom seeds

Wash the rice and leave to soak in water for an hour. Meanwhile fry the coconut in a little ghee until it begins to turn golden. Dissolve the sugar in two cups of water. Now boil the rice gently with the syrup and coconut milk until it begins to turn soft. Stir in the coconut and cardamom and cook until the rice is quite tender. Serve hot with cream or fruit.

Creamed Vermicelli (*Sevian*)

- 1 tablespoon ghee
- 6 cloves
- 6 cardamoms, skinned and crushed
- 1 cup broken vermicelli
- 3 cups milk
- 3 tablespoons sugar
- 1 tablespoon sultanas, fried in ghee
- 1 tablespoon almonds, blanched and sliced
- 1 tablespoon pistachios, ground

Heat the ghee, and gently fry the cloves and half the cardamom for two minutes. Add the vermicelli and fry until golden. Pour on the milk, bring to the boil and cook for ten minutes. Stir in the sugar, sultanas and nuts, and continue cooking until a nice thick mixture is obtained. Pour out into a dish and decorate with the rest of the cardamom and the ground pistachios. Serve hot or cold. Extra flavour and colour may be added by dissolving a pinch of saffron in a dessertspoon of rosewater and stirring into the nearly cooked savia (sevian). Some cooks prefer this dish to be dry, as they do the rice puddings. Simply continue cooking the mixture gently until the excess moisture has been driven off. Serve with cream. This dish is sometimes known as khir savia and is offered to Muslims at the end of a long fast since it is nourishing and easily digested.

Sweet Rice (*Mīthe chāval*)

Indian 'rice pudding' is served on festive occasions in Kashmir and served in small shallow earthenware pots. Children often find the best part of the pudding is the skin on the top and the caught layer on the bottom. In Kashmir the pudding is deliberately treated to produce these effects by setting the pot on hot coals and piling them on the lid also.

1 cup rice
1 cup sugar
1 cup water
6 cups milk
2 tablespoons ghee or butter
12 cardamoms
24 almonds, blanched and chopped
2 tablespoons sultanas, fried in ghee
pinch of saffron, dissolved in a little milk
1 tablespoon cashewnuts, finely chopped
1 tablespoon pistachios, ground

Wash the rice and leave to soak. Boil the sugar and water together for five minutes and add milk. Fry the drained rice in ghee for a few minutes until the grains become opaque. Cook the rice in the milk syrup until tender. Add the cardamoms, almonds, sultanas and saffron. When all the liquid is absorbed, transfer to a medium oven for half an hour. Serve sprinkled with the cashewnuts and pistachios.

Kerala Sweet Rice (*Naipayasam*)

1 cup rice
350 g (12 oz) grated jaggery or brown sugar
1 teaspoon powdered cardamom seeds
3–4 tablespoons ghee
½ cup grated coconut
1 tablespoon sultanas, fried in ghee
1 tablespoon cashewnuts, finely chopped

Wash the rice and cook in two cups of water until tender. Add the sugar and cardamom. As the sugar melts, stir in the ghee a spoonful at a time. When the rice is thick, remove from the heat and decorate with the coconut, sultanas and nuts. This payasam is a favourite offering to the goddess Durga.

Coconut Sweet Rice (*Mītha bhāt*)

1 cup rice
2 tablespoons ghee
4 cardamoms, crushed
4 cups coconut milk or creamed coconut
1 cup grated jaggery or brown sugar
pinch of saffron, dissolved in a little milk
1 tablespoon sultanas, fried in ghee
1 tablespoon cashewnuts, finely chopped

Wash the rice, drain and fry in ghee until the grains become opaque. Add the cardamoms and coconut milk and cook until the rice begins to become tender. Add the sugar and saffron, and continue cooking on a gentle heat until the mixture is thick and the rice is tender. Serve hot sprinkled with the sultanas and nuts. Mitha bhat is popular throughout Western India.

Sweet Saffron Rice (*Kesari bhāt*)

Shiva's wife may be known as Annapurna, the goddess who supplies all beings with food. In this aspect she is represented as sitting on a throne holding a ladle to dispense her bounty. She is sometimes worshipped by the bride when she is expecting her bridegroom to visit. She pours yellow rice on the image and asks the protection of the goddess for her guest.

2 cups rice
2 tablespoons ghee
6 caramoms, crushed
4 cups milk
1 cup brown sugar
1 cup peach slices
½ teaspoon saffron
1 tablespoon sultanas, fried in ghee
1 tablespoon almonds, blanched and sliced
1 tablespoon pistachios, ground

Wash the rice, drain and fry for a few minutes with the ghee. Throw in the cardamoms and pour on the milk. Cook gently until the rice begins to become tender. Stir in the sugar and fruit. Meanwhile dissolve half a teaspoon of saffron in half a cup of warm milk. When it is yellow, pour into the rice and continue cooking. When the rice is cooked, remove from the heat and garnish with the fried sultanas and nuts.

Tamil Festival Rice (*Pongal*)

The monthly entry of the sun into a zodiacal sign is called a *samkrānti*. The most important one is the winter solstice, the Makara Samkranti, when the sun enters Capricorn or Makara. This marks the beginning of the solar month of Magha and it is a time of great rejoicing. At Allahabad a great *mela* (fair) called the Magha Mela is held which lasts for a month. In South India this festival is called Pongal and it marks the start of the Tamil New Year. *Pongal* means 'boiled rice' in

Tamil and the word gives its name to the festival of Pongal which lasts for three days. During Pongal, khir is prepared from rice, milk and jaggery to be offered to Indra, who rules over the kingdom of the gods. This dish is served for breakfast. Rice at this time is cooked in new pots, and the coming year is said to be a prosperous one if the milk takes only a short time to boil. Cattle are venerated during Pongal, garlanded and fed with a thick rice gruel made with the juice of sugar cane.

2 cups rice
1 cup split green peas (mung dal)
1 litre (just under 2 pints) milk
2 cups grated jaggery or brown sugar
1 tablespoon sultanas, fried in ghee
1 tablespoon cashewnuts, chopped
1 cup ghee
4 cardamoms, powdered

Wash the rice and dal and put together in the milk. Cook on a gentle heat until tender and then add the sugar, sultanas and nuts. Stir in the ghee a spoonful at a time, remove from the heat and serve sprinkled with cardamom powder.

A simpler pongal known as Chakkarapongal is also offered in Tamilnadu temples. It is made in the following way:

28 g (1 oz) green gram (mung dal)
1500 ml (2½ pints) water
110 g (4 oz) jaggery or brown sugar
110 g (4 oz) rice
4 cardamoms, skinned and powdered
½ tablespoon cashewnuts, roasted
½ tablespoon grated coconut

Wash the dal and put in boiling water. Add the jaggery. When the dal is beginning to soften add the rice. When the grains are soft and the water is absorbed, add powdered cardamoms, cashewnuts and coconut and remove from the heat. Serve hot.

Krishna's Rice (*Palpayasam*)

1 cup rice
2 litres (3½ pints) milk
675 g (1½ lb) sugar

Wash the rice and boil gently in the milk until the mixture thickens (it should just spread when poured on to a plate). Add sugar and remove from heat. Stir thoroughly. This simple dessert is an offering favoured by Vishnu and Lord Krishna in Kerala temples.

Sweet Rice Pulau (*Zarda pulau*)

1½ cups rice
4 tablespoons ghee
6 cloves
6 cardamoms
small piece cinnamon
1 cup sugar
pinch of saffron, dissolved in a tablespoon hot milk
1 tablespoon sultanas, fried in ghee
1 tablespoon rosewater
1 tablespoon almonds, blanched and sliced
1 tablespoon pistachios, chopped
silver balls

Wash the rice and leave to soak. Drain. Heat the ghee, and gently fry the cloves, cardamoms and cinnamon for two minutes. Add the drained rice and continue frying until the grains become opaque. Pour on three cups of hot water and cook like a pulau until the rice is tender. Stir in the sugar and saffron. Mix well and stir in the sultanas, rosewater and half the nuts. Serve hot or cold garnished with the rest of the nuts and silver balls.

This recipe was known as Zardbiranj in the seventeenth century. In Nepal it is sometimes served topped with brown sugar and cream. Put the garnish on last of all.

Bengal Sweet Pulau

1½ cups rice
1 tablespoon cashewnuts, chopped
1 tablespoon almonds, blanched and sliced
1 tablespoon sultanas
4 tablespoons ghee
small piece ginger, finely chopped
4 cardamoms
4 cloves
small piece cinnamon
½ teaspoon caraway seeds
1 teaspoon cumin seeds
1 tablespoon khoya
1 tablespoon yogurt
pinch of saffron, dissolved in a tablespoon hot milk
1 tablespoon pistachios, ground

Wash the rice and leave to soak. Meanwhile gently fry the cashewnuts, almonds and sultanas in a little ghee. In a separate pan fry the drained rice in ghee with the ginger and other spices until the grains become opaque. Now mix in the khoya (see *khoya* under Basic Ingredients) and yogurt. Stir together well and pour on three cups of hot water, and allow the pulau to cook until the rice is nearly tender. Stir in the saffron. When the rice is tender serve garnished with the pistachios.

Creamed Rice Flour (*Firni*)

- 2½ tablespoons rice flour
- 1 litre (just under 2 pints) milk
- 4 tablespoons sugar
- 12 cardamoms, crushed
- 1 tablespoon almonds, blanched and sliced
- 1 tablespoon pistachios, ground

Mix the rice flour with enough milk to make a thin paste. Put in the rest of the milk and bring to the boil. Cook on a medium heat for fifteen minutes, stirring continuously. Add sugar and keep cooking for another ten minutes. By now the mixture should be fairly thick. Mix in the cardamom and almonds. Cook for a further five minutes. Pour into a bowl and garnish with the pistachios. Serve chilled. This recipe is from Northern India.

Fruit Firni

- 2½ tablespoons rice flour
- 1 litre (just under 2 pints) milk
- 4 tablespoons sugar
- pinch of saffron, dissolved in a tablespoon hot milk
- 2 cups chopped fruit
- 1 tablespoon cashewnuts chopped

Cook the firni as in the previous recipe, adding the saffron just before the end. Stir in well and cook for five minutes. Arrange the fruit in a dish and pour over the cooked firni. Garnish with nuts and serve chilled.

Condensed Milk Pudding (*Rabri*)

1 litre (just under 2 pints) full-cream milk
2 tablespoons sugar
1 teaspoon rosewater
1 tablespoon almonds, blanched and sliced
1 tablespoon pistachios, ground
6 cardamoms, skinned and powdered

Boil the milk, stirring continuously, until it is reduced to a quarter of the quantity. The equivalent in condensed milk could be used. Stir in the sugar. Remove from heat, allow to cool and stir in the rosewater. Pour into a dish and garnish with the nuts and cardamom. Serve chilled. This dish may be made more quickly by making the khoya in advance (see *khoya* under Basic Ingredients) although the taste will be slightly different.

Semolina Payesh (*Sūji payesh*)

2 tablespoons semolina
2 tablespoons ghee
3 cups milk
2 tablespoons brown sugar
4 cardamoms, skinned and powdered
1 tablespoon almonds, blanched and sliced
1 tablespoon cashewnuts, chopped
1 tablespoon pistachios, ground

Fry the semolina in ghee until it turns a light golden colour. Pour on the milk and mix in the sugar and cook until the mixture becomes thick. Stir in the cardamom, almonds and cashewnuts. Serve garnished with the pistachios.

Payesh are milk puddings from Bengal. What might be called khir in North-Western India may be called payesh or payas in Bengal.

Puli Payesh

250 g ($\frac{1}{2}$ lb) sweet potatoes, boiled, peeled and mashed
1 tablespoon wholewheat flour
6 cardamoms, skinned and powdered
750 ml ($1\frac{1}{2}$ pints) milk
$\frac{1}{2}$ cup brown sugar
1 tablespoon rosewater

Mix the sweet potatoes with the flour and cardamom powder and knead well. Form into small crescent shapes or pulis. Bring the milk to the boil, stir in the sugar and simmer gently. Put in the pulis carefully and continue cooking over a gentle heat until the mixture becomes thick. Remove from the heat and sprinkle on the rosewater. Serve chilled. Other similar vegetables may be used in this recipe such as yam, potato or green banana. The flour is used to bind when making the pulis.

Cheese Payesh (*Chenna payesh*)

1 litre (just under 2 pints) milk
½ cup sugar
250 g (½ lb) panir
6 cardamoms, skinned and powdered
1 tablespoon almonds, blanched and sliced
1 tablespoon sultanas, fried in ghee
1 tablespoon rosewater
1 tablespoon pistachios, ground

Bring the milk to the boil and lower the heat to simmer. Stir in the sugar and continue cooking until the milk is reduced to half the quantity. Mash the panir (see *panir* under Basic Ingredients) and stir in with the cardamom, almonds and sultanas and continue cooking until the mixture thickens a little more. Remove from the heat and allow to cool. Sprinkle on the rosewater and garnish with the pistachios.

South Indian Milk Pudding (*Payasam*)

1 cup rice
3 cups coconut milk or creamed coconut
½ cup grated jaggery or brown sugar
1 tablespoon cashewnuts, chopped and fried in ghee
1 teaspoon powdered cardamom seeds

Wash the rice and cook in the coconut milk until it begins to turn soft. Stir in the sugar, and continue cooking until the mixture thickens a little more and the rice is tender. Remove from the heat and serve garnished with the nuts and cardamom.

Gram Payasam

1 cup rice
½ cup green gram (mung dal) or other dal
2 tablespoons ghee
2 cups coconut milk or creamed coconut
1 cup grated jaggery or brown sugar
1 teaspoon powdered cardamom seeds
1 tablespoon cashewnuts
1 tablespoon sultanas

Wash the rice and dal and soak in water. Drain and fry in ghee until the grains of rice turn opaque. Add a cup of water and a cup of coconut milk and cook until the rice begins to turn soft. Stir in the sugar and cardamom and the rest of the coconut milk. Continue cooking on a gentle heat until the mixture turns thick. Meanwhile fry the nuts and sultanas in a little ghee, and use as a garnish for the payasam.

Banana Payasam

4 ripe bananas
1 cup grated jaggery or brown sugar
1 cup coconut milk or creamed coconut
1 teaspoon powdered cardamom seeds
½ cup grated coconut
1 tablespoon sultanas

Peel the bananas, put in a pan with a little water, and cook gently until the bananas are soft. Mash well. Meanwhile make a syrup by boiling the sugar with two cups of water. Add the mashed bananas and coconut milk, and cook until the mixture thickens. Stir in the cardamom powder and cook a little longer. Meanwhile fry the grated coconut and sultanas and use as a garnish.

Marrow Payasam

2 cups marrow, peeled and cubed
1 cup grated jaggery or brown sugar
1 cup coconut milk or creamed coconut
1 teaspoon powdered cardamom seeds
½ cup grated coconut
1 tablespoon cashewnuts
1 tablespoon sultanas

Put the marrow or similar vegetable in a pan with a little milk or water and cook gently until soft. Mash well. Meanwhile make a syrup by boiling the sugar with two cups of water. Add the mashed marrow and coconut milk and cook until the mixture thickens. Stir in the cardamom powder and cook a little longer. Meanwhile fry the grated coconut, nuts and sultanas in a little ghee and use to garnish the payasam.

Mango Payasam

Use the same amount of fruit as in the previous recipe. Peaches are a good substitute if mangoes are unavailable. Cook the payasam in the same way.

Cream Cheese Balls (*Ras malai*)

Make rasgullas (see Curd Balls under Sweets in Syrup) and prepare a filling:

1 tablespoon double cream	2 cups water
1 teaspoon pistachios, ground	4 cups milk
1 teaspoon ground almonds	½ cup double cream
2 teaspoons sugar	1 tablespoon rosewater
1 cup sugar	1 tablespoon pistachios, ground

Mix up the tablespoon of cream with the pistachios, almonds and sugar. Flatten the cheese balls and make a depression in each. Fill with the mixture and roll up again. Make a syrup by boiling the sugar and water for a few minutes and gently cook the balls in it for ten minutes. Remove and leave to soak in the milk for 3–4 hours. Remove and drain. Now make the milk into rabri by heating and reducing to half the quantity. Stir in the double cream. Pour over the flattened cheese balls, sprinkle with rosewater and garnish with pistachios. Serve chilled. This is a favourite dessert in Bengal.

Sweet Curd (*Shrīkand*)

The cowherd (*gopa*) of Mughal times took rice and curds along with vegetables and *Sikhram* which was made of curd, sugar, grated coconut and saffron. Shrikand is made all over India with local variations in ingredients. This recipe comes from Gujerat and is served with hot breads such as puris. It is an extremely nourishing and tasty dessert.

4 cups yogurt
pinch of saffron
1 tablespoon rosewater
1 cup sugar
10 cardamoms, skinned and powdered
1 tablespoon almonds, blanched and sliced
1 tablespoon pistachios, ground

Put the yogurt in a muslin bag or cloth and allow to hang overnight so that the excess moisture drips off. Next day scrape out the thickened curd. Dissolve the saffron in the rosewater and beat into the curd. Mix in the sugar, cardamom and almonds and beat again. Garnish with the pistachios and serve chilled.

In Nepal, cloves, cinnamon and pepper are added with the cardamom to give a more spicy flavour.

Banana in Curd (*Kela raita*)

4–6 ripe bananas
3 cups yogurt
2 tablespoons brown sugar
4 cardamoms, skinned and powdered

Peel the bananas and mash well. Beat into the yogurt with the rest of the ingredients. Serve with hot sweet breads.

Sultanas in Curd (*Kishmish raita*)

4 tablespoons sultanas
2 tablespoons ghee
3 cups yogurt
2 tablespoons brown sugar
pinch of saffron, dissolved in a tablespoon warm milk
1 tablespoon pistachios, ground

Fry the sultanas in ghee until they puff up. Do not allow them to burn. Beat into the yogurt with the sugar and saffron. Garnish with pistachios and serve with hot sweet breads.

Peach in Curd (*Arū raita*)

3 large peaches or other similar fruit
3 cups yogurt
2 tablespoons brown sugar
½ cup grated coconut
½ teaspoon fennel seeds, ground
1 tablespoon pistachios, ground

Peel the fruit and cut in cubes. Beat the curd and stir in the sugar, coconut and fennel seed. Mix in the fruit pieces and garnish with pistachios. Serve with hot sweet breads.

Semolina Pudding (*Sūji halva*)

4 tablespoons ghee
1 tablespoon sultanas
1 cup semolina (suji)
4 cardamoms, skinned and powdered
1 cup sugar
4 cloves
small piece cinnamon
3 cups water
1 tablespoon rosewater
1 tablespoon cashewnuts, chopped
1 tablespoon pistachios, ground

Heat ghee, and fry the sultanas and semolina until the semolina is golden, stirring continuously. Add the cardamom, sugar, cloves, cinnamon and water. Mix well and cook gently for a further fifteen minutes. When all the excess water has been driven off, pour into a dish. Sprinkle with rosewater and decorate with nuts. Serve hot or cold.

Gujerati Milk Pudding (*Shīra*)

3 tablespoons wholewheat flour
2 tablespoons ghee
2 cups milk
2 tablespoons brown sugar
6 cardamoms, skinned and powdered
1 tablespoon sesame seeds, ground
10 almonds, blanched and sliced
1 tablespoon pistachios, ground

Sieve the flour and fry in ghee until it turns golden. Pour on the milk and stir well. Add the sugar, cardamom, sesame and almonds and cook until the mixture turns quite thick. Serve hot garnished with the pistachios. This shira, like khir and payas, is sometimes served more milky. Simply add more milk.

Sweet Corn Shira

2 corn cobs
2 tablespoons ghee
2 cups milk
2 tablespoons brown sugar
6 cardamoms, skinned and powdered
1 tablespoon sesame seeds, ground
pinch of saffron, dissolved in a tablespoon warm milk
1 tablespoon pistachios, ground

Choose the corn cobs carefully. Pull back the green leaves to expose the corn. They should be fat and golden and if broken should give out a milky juice. Take off the corn from the cobs and mash well. Lightly fry in ghee. Add the milk and stir well. Add the sugar, cardamom, sesame and saffron and cook the mixture until it turns quite thick. Serve hot garnished with the pistachios. Again, the dish may be served more milky.

Green Gram Shira

1 cup green gram (mung dal) or other dal
4 tablespoons ghee
2 cloves
small piece cinnamon
4 cardamoms
2 cups milk
2 tablespoons brown sugar
1 tablespoon sesame seeds, ground
1 tablespoon sultanas, fried in ghee
1 tablespoon cashewnuts, chopped
1 tablespoon rosewater
1 tablespoon pistachios, ground

Wash the dal and leave to soak for an hour. Drain and fry in ghee with the spices until the dal turns golden. Pour on the milk and stir well. Add the sugar, sesame, sultanas and cashewnuts, and cook on a gentle heat until the mixture turns quite thick. Remove from the heat, sprinkle on the rosewater and garnish with the pistachios.

Coconut Shira

4 tablespoons semolina
ghee
2 cups coconut milk or creamed coconut
2 tablespoons brown sugar
4 tablespoons grated coconut
6 cardamoms, skinned and powdered
1 tablespoon cashewnuts, chopped
1 tablespoon sultanas, fried in ghee

Fry the semolina in two tablespoons of ghee until it begins to turn golden. Pour on the coconut milk and stir well. Add the sugar, cook the mixture on a gentle heat. Meanwhile gently fry the coconut and stir into the shira. Add the cardamom, cashewnuts and sultanas, and continue cooking until the mixture turns quite thick. Serve hot with sweet breads. This shira is from Western India.

Peach Shira

4 tablespoons semolina
2 tablespoons ghee
2 cups milk
2 tablespoons sugar
6 cardamoms, skinned and powdered
1 tablespoon almonds, blanched and sliced
1 tablespoon cashewnuts, chopped
2–3 peaches, peeled and sliced
1 tablespoon sultanas, fried in ghee

Fry the semolina in ghee until it begins to turn golden. Pour on the milk and stir well. Add the sugar, cardamom, almonds and cashewnuts, and continue cooking over a gentle heat until the mixture begins to turn thick. Carefully put in the peach slices. Cook to make a thick mixture and serve garnished with the sultanas.

Banana Pudding (*Bhareli keli*)

4–6 large bananas
1 cup grated coconut
½ cup grated jaggery or brown sugar
8 cardamoms, skinned and powdered
1 tablespoon cashewnuts, finely chopped
2 cups coconut milk or creamed coconut
1 tablespoon pistachios, ground

Peel the bananas and slice down the middle. Arrange the slices in a baking dish. Mix together the coconut, sugar, cardamom and cashewnuts. Spread the mixture over the sliced bananas and pour the coconut milk over the whole. Bake in a low oven until most of the moisture is absorbed and the bananas are well cooked. Serve garnished with the pistachios. This dish is delicious with cream or rabri (see Rabri under this section).

Peach and Coconut Pudding

- 2 tablespoons rice flour or corn flour
- 2 tablespoons sugar
- 1 cup peach slices with their juice
- 1 cup milk
- ½ cup grated coconut
- 1 tablespoon almonds, blanched and sliced, fried in ghee

Mix the rice flour, sugar and peach together, and cook over a gentle heat until they are well blended. Add the milk and coconut, and stir well. Continue cooking for another ten minutes, stirring continuously until the pudding becomes quite thick. Pour into a dish and serve garnished with the almonds.

Drinks

The moon, being a reservoir of nectar, gives out nectarine rays. In some parts, sweet drinks are exposed to these rays during the whole of the night of the full-moon of Ashvin (September–October) in order to absorb them. Next morning these drinks are quaffed in the belief that many complaints and diseases, especially those affecting the eyes, will be cured. Sweets so exposed, it is said, should be kept in an air-tight jar and small pieces eaten every morning to gain strength and to improve the complexion.

Nourishers

This section includes nourishing restoratives, pick-me-ups and drinks. They are especially good for anyone engaged in exercise, prolonged mental effort or recovering from illness.

Almond Restorer

4 tablespoons almonds, blanched
4 tablespoons brown sugar
2 tablespoons fresh orange juice
1 litre (just under 2 pints) water

Grind the almonds with the sugar. Add a little orange juice to make a smooth paste. Put in a bowl with the rest of the orange juice and pour on the rest of the water. Leave to stand before serving.

Honey Milk

1 cup milk
2 teaspoons honey
pinch of cardamom powder or nutmeg

Heat the milk but do not allow to boil. Stir in the honey and serve sprinkled with cardamom. This may be drunk hot as a nourishing day-time drink or nightcap, or chill to make a refresher. A quick nourishing drink may be prepared by stirring liquid honey into a glass of milk. Top with powdered nuts and stir well.

Nut Milk

½ tablespoon almonds, blanched
½ tablespoon cashewnuts
3 cups milk
honey or brown sugar
crystallized fruit
1 tablespoon pistachios, ground

Grind the nuts to a paste and stir into the milk. Stir in the sugar or honey to taste and beat until frothy. Top with finely chopped crystallized fruit and pistachios.

Coconut Milk

1 cup coconut milk or creamed coconut
1 cup milk
1 tablespoon cream or evaporated milk
grated coconut
ground pistachios

Mix the coconut milk (see under Basic Ingredients) with the milk and beat until frothy. Top with cream and grated coconut and a sprinkling of pistachio.

Buttermilk

For two glasses of buttermilk, mix together a teaspoonful of chopped fresh ginger, a tablespoon of honey, half a teaspoon of powdered cardamom seeds. Pound together and stir into the buttermilk. Allow to settle before drinking. Caraway seeds may be substituted for the cardamom for a slightly different taste.

Curd Drink (*Lassi*)

To make 1 glass:

Beat half a glass of yogurt with half a glass of cold water. Add sugar to taste if required. Serve chilled in summer. Lassi is one of the most popular drinks in India. Simply make combinations of yogurt, water, herbs and flavourings to create your own lassi. A very good thirst-quencher in the hot months can be made by beating a tablespoon of yogurt with a glass of water. Put in ice and a few drops of lime juice or lemon juice.

Fruit Lassi

1 cup yogurt
2 teaspoons honey
juice of a lemon
½ cup finely chopped soft fruit
1 cup water

Beat the yogurt and mix in all the ingredients thoroughly. Serve decorated with flower petals.

Vegetable Squash

1 carrot
1 onion
½ cup peas
2 tomatoes

Put the vegetables in a liquidizer. Add a pinch of salt and brown sugar and a little water if necessary, as you liquidize. Serve chilled with a garnish of finely chopped mint leaf. If a liquidizer is not available, cut the vegetables into small pieces and cook with a little water. When tender, mash well with the liquid, strain and add water. Frequently the liquid from cooking vegetables is discarded. Try keeping some and mixing in some herbs and sugar to make a vegetable drink, thus conserving the nourishment that might have been thrown away.

Tomato Squash

To each glass of tomato juice, add a teaspoon of finely chopped celery, a teaspoon of lemon juice, a teaspoon of brown sugar and a teaspoon of finely chopped spring onion. Allow the ingredients to settle or strain and chill before serving.

Semolina Restorer (*Sūji conji*)

1 tablespoon semolina
ghee
4 cups milk
pinch of salt
2 teaspoons brown sugar

Grease a hot plate or pan, and lightly roast the semolina until it begins to turn golden. Stir into a pan of milk with the salt and sugar and boil until the semolina is cooked. Serve hot or cold.

Fenugreek Restorer (*Methi conji*)

2 teaspoons fenugreek seeds
½ cup rice
pinch of salt
1 cup coconut milk or creamed coconut
brown sugar

Steep the seeds in half a cup of water overnight. Wash the rice and leave to soak for the same time. Next day boil the seeds in a cup of water until soft. Add the drained rice, two cups of water and salt. Cook on a gentle heat until the rice is soft. Pour in the coconut milk and stir in sugar to taste. Ordinary milk may be substituted for the coconut milk.

Wheat Restorer (*Ātā conji*)

1 cup crushed wheat
3 cups water
1 cup coconut milk or creamed coconut
2 cardamoms, skinned and crushed
brown sugar

Wash the wheat and boil gently with water until the grains are soft, adding more water if necessary. Add the coconut milk, cardamom and sugar to taste. These conjis are from Maharashtra.

Refreshers

These are excellent drinks in hot weather, after exercise, returning from shopping or a tiring day at work.

Mango Refresher

The mango flower is offered to the moon, to whom it is held sacred, on the second day of Magh. The mango is also sacred to Madan, the Indian equivalent of Cupid. Mango leaves are used to festoon halls and other places where marriages and similar auspicious ceremonies take place. On Mahashivaratra day, Shiva is worshipped with mango blossom.

- 2 cups tinned mango or boiled fresh mango
- 2 glasses water
- 2 tablespoons brown sugar
- 2 teaspoons rosewater
- ½ teaspoon cumin powder

Mash the mango well and mix with the water. Strain and mix in the rest of the ingredients. Serve chilled.

Ginger and Lemon Refresher

- ½ tablespoon chopped fresh ginger
- 4 tablespoons brown sugar
- juice of 1 lemon
- 2 glasses of water

Pound the ginger with sugar and mix together with the rest of the ingredients. Allow to settle and serve chilled garnished with finely chopped mint leaf.

Tamarind Refresher

- 1 tablespoon tamarind pulp
- juice of 1 lemon
- 4 tablespoons brown sugar
- 2 cardamoms, skinned and powdered

Soak the tamarind in a glass of hot water and leave for a few hours. Strain. Mix in the rest of the ingredients. Serve chilled topped with a little finely chopped mint leaf.

Brown Sugar Refresher

110 g (4 oz) brown sugar
juice of 1 lemon
2 cardamoms, skinned and powdered

Melt the sugar in two glasses of water. Stir in the lemon juice and cardamom. Serve chilled, topped with tiny flower petals. Treacle, jaggery or honey may be used in this recipe.

Mint and Lemon Refresher

2 tablespoons fresh mint leaves
1 tablespoon chopped fresh ginger
juice of 1 lemon
sugar

Pound the mint leaves and ginger, and pour on two glasses of hot water. Stir well and leave to soak for half an hour. Strain and mix in the lemon juice and sugar to taste. Serve chilled, topped with a little finely chopped mint leaf.

Orange and Lemon Refresher

2 oranges
1 lemon
1 tablespoon brown sugar or honey
pinch of salt

Squeeze the juice from the oranges and lemon, and mix with the sugar. Salt is optional but helps to point up the taste of the fruit juice. Serve chilled, topped with a few flower petals.

Lemon Water (*Nimbū pāni*)

juice of 3 lemons
1½ tablespoons sugar
3 teaspoons rosewater

Mix the lemon juice and sugar until the sugar dissolves. Add four glasses of water and stir in the rosewater. Serve chilled, topped with finely chopped mint leaf or thin slices of lemon.

Cumin Water (*Jāl jīra*)

4 tablespoons tamarind pulp
4 tablespoons mint leaf, chopped
½ teaspoon cumin powder
pinch chilli powder
pinch of salt
brown sugar

Soak the tamarind pulp in six glasses of hot water for an hour and strain off the juice. Grind the mint with the rest of the ingredients and stir into the tamarind water. Add salt and sugar to taste. This drink can be served as an appetizer either hot or cold. It is very nice served chilled in the summer.

Melon Sherbet

2 cups melon pulp
2–3 tablespoons sugar
2 cardamoms, skinned and powdered
2 teaspoons rosewater

This is an excellent way of utilizing an over-ripe melon. Add two glasses of soda water or water to the pulp and stir in the sugar, cardamom and rosewater. Strain if necessary and serve chilled. Other ripe soft fruit may be treated in the same way.

Tamarind Sherbet

½ tablespoon chopped fresh ginger
1 tablespoon tamarind pulp
small piece cinnamon
pinch of salt
2 teaspoons brown sugar
soda water

Pound the ginger and tamarind in a bowl with the cinnamon and salt. Pour on 3 cups of boiling water. Stir to break up the pulp. Leave to stand until cold. Strain. Add the sugar and serve diluted with soda water.

Almond Sherbet

4 tablespoons almonds
2 cups brown sugar
8 cardamoms, skinned and powdered
1 tablespoon rosewater
a few drops of almond essence

Blanch the almonds in hot water and cool. Peel and grind to a paste. Mix the sugar with a cup of hot water and allow to dissolve. Stir in the almond paste, cardamom, rosewater and almond essence. Serve diluted with soda water.

Rose Sherbet

1 heaped tablespoon rosepetals
2 cups sugar
2 tablespoons rosewater

Soak petals overnight in a cup of water. Strain. Dissolve the sugar in a cup of hot water, pour in the rose extract and boil until the syrup begins to thicken. Add the rosewater after cooling. Serve with soda water, topped with tiny rose petals.

Aniseed Tea

4 tablespoons aniseed or fennel seed
4 cups black tea

Boil the aniseed or fennel seed in two cups of water until tender and the water is well aromatized. Strain into the tea. Add milk and sugar according to taste and serve in glasses. Aniseed tea may also be served chilled.

Kashmiri Tea (*Kahva*)

- 2½ cups milk + 2½ cups water *or* 5 cups water
- 3 level teaspoons green tea
- 1 teaspoon Darjeeling or Orange Pekoe Tea
- 6 cardamoms
- 6 almonds, blanched and chopped
- small piece cinnamon
- 2 cloves

Stew the ingredients gently for 15–30 minutes. Strain and serve hot, adding sugar to taste. Kashmiri sweet tea is sometimes additionally perfumed with saffron. It is made in a samovar and, like the Tibetans and the people of the frontier countries, the Kashmiris enjoy tea-drinking at any time of day or night.

The Master's Tale

The beggars all agreed that the snake-charmer had been singularly unlucky. 'Why didn't you get some more snakes?' asked one of them.

'I felt it was a sign,' replied the snake-charmer beggar. 'Besides, my mother wouldn't hear of it.'

'Well at least today we can say we have all been entertained like kings!' exclaimed the cripple, who had now lost his cynical tone.

Deviprasad's master looked at him. 'I am pleased that you feel so, since it is you all who have made me into a king. It is true enough that we are all beggars and cripples of a sort. I do not mean this as an insult, I mean that we can all learn from one another. Listening to you this evening reminds me of a day during my childhood when I and a few friends were playing at being king. We had been quarrelling, I seem to remember, over who was to be king that day when we suddenly noticed the appearance of a man dressed in poor cloth. His smile was kindly and he asked if he might settle the argument. We told him it was about being king for the day. He chuckled at this and said he knew a good way to find out who was worthy. He would set us a task to test us, he said. It sounded exciting, so we all agreed to this.

'Each of us had to run to the other end of the village and look at a hut standing on its own, and then report what we had seen to the stranger. One by one we set off. One of us very carefully described the dimensions of the hut while another described what it was made of. The next boy came back and said he had seen someone sitting inside the doorway. It was a woman holding a child in her arms and the child was crying, he said. Then we had to wait a little while for the last of us to return.

'"I'm sorry to have kept you waiting, sir," he said to the stranger, "but I saw this lady sitting in the hut you asked us to look at. I went up to her and saw she was nursing a sick child which kept crying all the time. I asked her why the child was sick and she said she was too poor to buy milk which the child needed and she could not ask anyone in our village for help. My mother had given me a coin yesterday for picking fruit so I ran to the milk-seller and bought some for her."

'Then our friend looked down rather shamefaced. "I'm sorry, but I can't tell you much about the hut because I forgot all about it."

'I wanted to laugh at this and I saw the stranger was smiling too. "You have done well. A king needs to know how to calculate and measure. He also requires knowledge of many subjects and he needs to be vigilant when he journeys round his realm to see that all is well. But most of all, a king needs to be kind and thoughtful. So I award the crown to the last one home who not only noticed the poor woman and her child, but was kind and thoughtful to them also."'

As Deviprasad's master finished the tale, the beggars burst out with their applause.

Note on Pronunciation of Indian Words

Indian languages are written phonetically and all the letters are pronounced. Except for 'ch' and 'sh', an 'h' after a consonant should be pronounced separately. 'E' and 'o' are long vowels; 'i' is pronounced long at the end of a word.

Pronounce 'a' as 'u' in the English word 'but'
'ā' as 'a' in the English word 'father'
'i' as 'i' in the English word 'bit'
'ī' as 'ee' in the English word 'meet'
'u' as 'oo' in the English word 'book'
'ū' as 'oo' in the English word 'moon'

You will notice a variation in English transliteration of Indian words amongst authors and on the menus of restaurants. This is partly due to the phonetic nature of Indian language alphabets and local changes in pronunciation. Long vowels may sometimes appear as double letters. For example 'moong daal' for 'mūng dāl'.

Glossary

ālū	potato
arū	peach
avidya	ignorance (Sanskrit)
badām	almond
barfi	milk sweetmeat
batāta	potato
bāth	South Indian rice dish
besan	gram flour (see Basic Ingredients)
Bhagavad Gītā	'The Song of the Lord', part of the *Mahābhārata* that contains the teachings of Krishna
channa	yellow peas
chapāti	flat bread made from wholewheat flour and water
chāval	rice
chenna	curd cheese (see Basic Ingredients), used especially in Bengali sweets
conji	thick nourishing gruel or soup
dāl	split peas
dosa	South Indian pancake
dūdh	milk
gājar	carrot
ghee	clarified butter (ghi) (see Basic Ingredients)
gūda	marrow
gur	jaggery, raw unprocessed sugar
halva	thick, jelly-like sweetmeat made by reducing fruit or vegetable with sugar
idli	dumpling
jaggery	gur, raw unprocessed sugar bought in a lump
jāmun	plum, plum-shaped milk sweetmeat (jāman)
jīra	cumin
kela	banana

khīr	a technique of creaming by cooking in milk, also shīra, shīr, payas, payesh
khoya	thick milk made by slowly driving off the water (see Basic Ingredients)
kishmish	sultana
laddū	sweetmeat in form of a ball, often made with gram flour
Lalitāsahasranāman	the Thousand Names of the Divine Mother or goddess Lalita is a devotional text used as a book of praise
lassi	refreshing drink made with yogurt
malai	cream
masūr dāl	red lentils
mīthe	sweet
mūng dāl	green lentils
nareal	coconut
nimbu	lime, lemon
pak	often a fudge-like sweetmeat (Gujerat)
pāni	water (North India)
panir	hard cheese made from curd (see Basic Ingredients)
parātha	flat bread made from wholewheat flour and fried in ghee, often stuffed
payesh	milk dessert like khir or shira, also payasam in South India
pistā	pistachio
poli, puli	see *pūri*
pūja	worship, whether public or private
pulau	rice first fried in ghee, then cooked in a stock which should be fully absorbed
pūri	small puffed breads fried in ghee, made with various flours
raita	vegetable or fruit in curd (North India)
rajas	in Indian philosophy, the quality of action (Sanskrit)
ras	rose
roti	bread
samosa	puffed pastry with filling
sattva	In Indian philosophy, the quality of harmony (Sanskrit)
savia, sevian	vermicelli
sūji	semolina
tamas	in Indian philosophy, the quality of inertia (Sanskrit)

tava	Indian concave iron dish used as a hot plate
til	sesame seed, has a sweet oil
urhad dāl	black or white gram lentils
vadi	fudge-like sweetmeat (Maharashtra)

Where to Buy Indian Ingredients

WEST

*Bazaar of India, 1331 University Avenue, Berkeley, California 94702
*Bezjian's Grocery, 4725 Santa Monica Blvd.,
Los Angeles, California 90029
California Direct Import Co. (Oh's), 2651 Mission St.,
San Francisco, California 94110
*Haig's Delicacies, 642 Clement St., San Francisco, California 94118
*India Imports & Exports, 10641 West Pico Blvd.,
Los Angeles, California 90064
*Porter's Food Unlimited, 125 West 11th St., Eugene, Oregon 97401
*Specialty Spice Shop; mail order address: 2757 152nd Avenue, N.E.,
Redmond, Washington 98052; retail outlet: Pike Place Market,
Seattle, Washington 98101
*Tarver's Delicacies, De Anza Shopping Center,
1338 South Mary Avenue, Sunnyvale, California 94087
Wholy Foods, 2999 Shattuck Avenue, Berkeley, California 94705

MIDWEST

*India Gift and Food Store, 1031 Belmont, Chicago, Illinois 60657
*International House of Foods, 440 West Gorham St.,
Madison, Wisconsin 53703

SOUTH

*Antone's, 2606 South Sheridan, Tulsa, Oklahoma 74129
*Jay Store, 4023 Westheimer, Houston, Texas 77027
Jung's Oriental Foods and Gifts,
2519 North Fitzburgh, Dallas, Texas 75204
Yoga and Health Center, 2912 Oaklawn, Dallas, Texas 75222

EAST

*Aphrodisia, 28 Carmine St., New York, New York 10014
*House of Spices, 76-17 Broadway, Jackson Heights, New York 11373
*India Food and Gourmet, 110 Lexington Ave.,
New York, New York 10016
*Indian Super Bazaar; mail order address: P.O. Box 1977, Silver Spring,
Maryland 20902; retail outlets: 3735 Rhode Island, Mt. Rainier,
20822; International Bazaar, 7720 Wisconsin Avenue, Bethesda, 20014
*Kalpana Indian Groceries, 4275 Main St., Flushing, New York 11355
*K. Kalustyan, Orient Export Trading Corp., 123 Lexington Ave.,
New York, New York 10016
T. G. Koryn, Inc., 66 Broad St., Carlstad, New Jersey 07072
*Spice Corner, 904 South 9th, Philadelphia, Pennsylvania 19147
*Spices and Foods Unlimited, Inc., 2018 A Florida Ave., N.W.,
Washington D.C. 20009

CANADA

*T. Eaton's Co., 190 Yonge St., Toronto 205, Ontario
*S. Enkin Inc., Imports and Exports,
1201 St. Lawrence, Montreal 18, Quebec

*these will mail order